The Substitute
Source Book
Cross-Curricular Activities

Art

Science

Math

Health

English

Environment

by Kevin Rigg

Mrs. N. Pitre

Published with the permission of R.I.C. Publications Pty. Ltd.

Copyright © 2006 by Didax, Inc., Rowley, MA 01969. All rights reserved.

First published by R.I.C. Publications Pty. Ltd., Perth, Western Australia. Revised by Didax Educational Resources.

Printed in the United States of America.

Order Number 2-5269
ISBN 1-58324-249-X

A B C D E F 10 09 08 07 06

395 Main Street
Rowley, MA 01969
www.worldteacherspress.com

Foreword

The Substitute Source is a series of four books which provides convenient resources to assist substitute teachers with classroom planning and organization on a long-term basis. The reproducible worksheets cover the learning areas of English, mathematics, science, health, society and environment, technology and the arts. The series is also a valuable resource for the classroom teacher, as the worksheets may be used to introduce, consolidate, or assess topics being taught.

Additional titles available in this series:

The Substitute Source Book (Grades 1–2)

The Substitute Source Book (Grades 3–4)

The Substitute Source Book (Grades 7–8)

Internet Web Sites

In some cases, Web sites or specific URLs may be recommended. While these are checked and rechecked at the time of publication, the publisher has no control over any subsequent changes which may be made to Web pages. It is strongly recommended that the class teacher checks all URLs before allowing students to access them.

View all pages online
Web site: www.worldteacherspress.com

Contents

Teacher Information

The worksheets can all be used as single lessons if time is limited, or they may be extended by including some additional activities to expand the topic into other curriculum areas. In some cases, it is possible to develop an entire day's work around one lesson sheet.

The theme pack at the end of each book is an ideal springboard for a long-term substitute assignment, yet each worksheet within the theme pack can stand alone as an individual lesson. The "Insects" theme pack in this book covers the learning areas of English, mathematics, science and technology.

The lessons have been specifically designed for the targeted grade levels. Worksheets from the same section of another book in the series may be more appropriate for any student who is working at a different level from the rest of the class. In many cases, the worksheets are differentiated by outcome rather than task, and so are appropriate for more than one level of ability.

A number of different teaching methods are included throughout the series to assist in the development of a range of skills across all learning areas.

Each lesson has detailed teacher notes which include:

- *Learning area covered.*
- *Strand(s) of the learning area.*
- *Indicators, summarizing what the students may achieve.*
- *A list of resources required, beyond those normally available in the classroom.*
- *Specific Web sites relevant to the activity, where appropriate.*
- *A detailed lesson plan, including ideas for classroom organization.*
- *Additional activities which extend the theme and expand it into other curriculum areas, including ideas for display.*
- *Answers, where necessary.*

A printed record sheet is provided for the teacher to keep account of which lessons have been completed with specific classes. A blank copy of the sheet is also included for the teacher to keep his/her own records.

If the worksheets are used for assessment purposes, the lesson plan and organization provided on the teacher's page may not be appropriate, and an alternative strategy may need to be employed.

It is assumed that normal classroom stationery and basic art and craft resources are readily available; for example, pencils, scissors and glue.

Some lessons require the students to access information and resources from home. Such cases should be communicated to the students prior to the day of the lesson.

When possible, audio and video recordings could be made and photographs taken to increase student motivation and encourage students to perform at their best level. These may be used as evidence of work and as resources to be used at other times. The photographs may be used to enhance displays of work.

It is recommended that substitute teachers keep a selection of samples of work from this book as a record of their substitute teaching experience.

Display/Presentation Ideas

Teachers completing a short term of substitute teaching may not find it necessary to display worksheets from these books. However, teachers completing long-term assignments, or classroom teachers may find some of these display/presentation ideas useful:

- *Staple worksheets back to back and hang over string/wire suspended across the room.*
- *Select the most appropriate worksheets to display around a shape, poster, rhyme, or picture relating to the worksheets.*
- *Combine all the worksheets to form a book with a cover for the class library.*
- *Display worksheets with artwork by selected students.*
- *Fix worksheets to an appropriate frieze painted by the students.*
- *Students decorate the border of the worksheet with relevant shapes or pictures.*
- *Students create an artwork or shape relevant to the worksheet and attach their worksheet to it. The artwork/shape should be larger than the worksheet (Poster size).*

Teacher Pages

A teacher page accompanies each student worksheet. Each provides the following information:

The symbol at the top indicates the learning area.

The title indicates the activity being covered.

The indicators summarize what the students may achieve on completion of the task.

The strand(s) indicate which dominant part or parts of the learning area are being focused upon. Other strands may also be incorporated into a lesson, such as writing or reading.

The resources list those requirements for the task which might not normally be readily available in the classroom. Teachers may select those which are appropriate or easy to obtain.

These may include items and information which students bring from home, library resources on a particular topic, magazines for cutting out pictures, literature relevant to the activity, prepared work and resources to demonstrate what is required from students or to help with class discussion. Any prepared work and resources may be kept and used for future lessons.

The lesson plan and organization provides a detailed structure for the lesson and ideas for classroom organization.

Most lessons begin with a discussion to determine how much the students already know about the subject. Some resources may be used at this stage to enhance discussion.

Reading through the worksheet with the students ensures they understand what is required of them. Allowing students to work in small groups to discuss their work and, where necessary, to prepare and edit drafts, gives them the opportunity to learn from one another.

The additional activities provide suggestions for extending the activity and expanding it into other curriculum areas.

These activities include suggestions for display, ideas for research and projects, designing and playing games, dramatizing roles, conducting surveys and presenting results graphically.

The answers are provided as necessary. In many cases, it is expected that the students' work will be teacher checked.

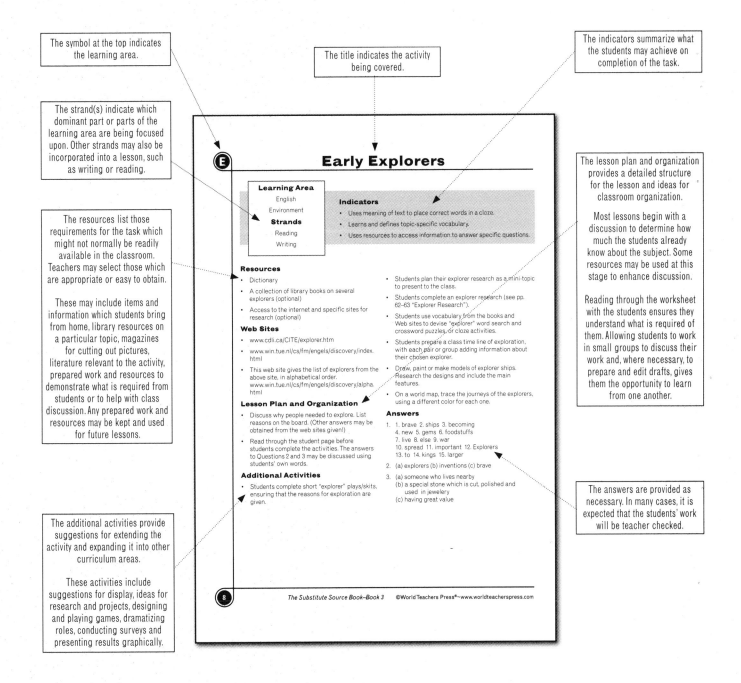

Early Explorers

Learning Area
English
Environment
Strands
Reading
Writing

Indicators
- Uses meaning of text to place correct words in a cloze.
- Learns and defines topic-specific vocabulary.
- Uses resources to access information to answer specific questions.

Resources
- Dictionary
- A collection of library books on several explorers (optional)
- Access to the internet and specific sites for research (optional)

Web Sites
- www.cdli.ca/CITE/explorer.htm
- www.win.tue.nl/cs/fm/engels/discovery/index.html
- This web site gives the list of explorers from the above site, in alphabetical order. www.win.tue.nl/cs/fm/engels/discovery/alpha.html

Lesson Plan and Organization
- Discuss why people needed to explore. List reasons on the board. (Other answers may be obtained from the web sites given!)
- Read through the student page before students complete the activities. The answers to Questions 2 and 3 may be discussed using students' own words.

Additional Activities
- Students complete short "explorer" plays/skits, ensuring that the reasons for exploration are given.

- Students plan their explorer research as a mini-topic to present to the class.
- Students complete an explorer research (see pp. 62–63 "Explorer Research").
- Students use vocabulary from the books and Web sites to devise "explorer" word search and crossword puzzles, or cloze activities.
- Students prepare a class time line of exploration, with each pair or group adding information about their chosen explorer.
- Draw, paint or make models of explorer ships. Research the designs and include the main features.
- On a world map, trace the journeys of the explorers, using a different color for each one.

Answers
1. 1. brave 2. ships 3. becoming
   4. new 5. gems 6. foodstuffs
   7. live 8. else 9. war
   10. spread 11. important 12. Explorers
   13. to 14. kings 15. larger

2. (a) explorers (b) inventions (c) brave

3. (a) someone who lives nearby
   (b) a special stone which is cut, polished and used in jewelery
   (c) having great value

8 *The Substitute Source Book–Book 3* ©World Teachers Press®~www.worldteacherspress.com

Student Worksheets

The student worksheets provide a range of activities to assist in the development of skills across all learning areas of the curriculum.

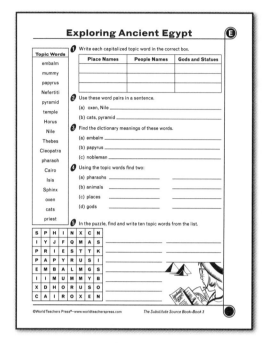

English
Exploring Ancient Egypt (page 27)

Students extract information about the topic from a range of sources. They use dictionary skills to find word definitions and demonstrate their understanding of topic words by using them in a sentence.

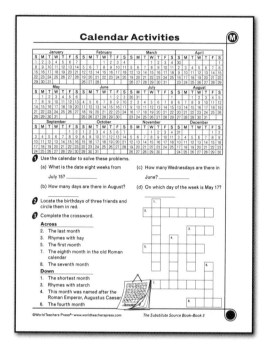

Mathematics
Calendar Activities (page 53)

Students use a calendar to solve problems. They understand that the months of the year do not all have the same number of days. They learn something about the history of the calendar.

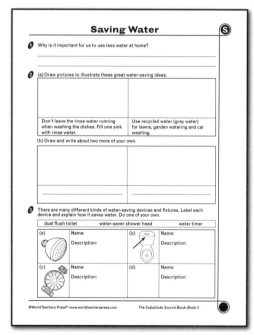

Science
Saving Water (page 61)

Students understand the value of each person reducing his/her use of water for the benefit of all . They consider ways in which water use may be reduced and learn about the development of water-saving devices.

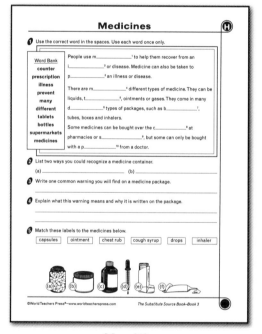

Health
Medicines (page 65)

Students understand that medicines come in a range of packaging. They appreciate the need for safety features in packaging and realize the dangers of misusing medicines.

The Substitute Source Book–Book 3

Student Worksheets

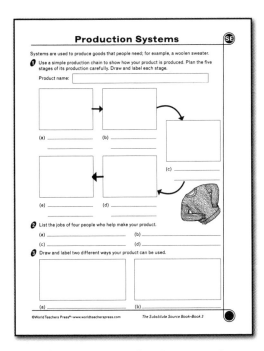

Society and Environment
Production Systems (page 71)

Students demonstrate their awareness of the natural changes that occur with the seasons and how these affect their life.

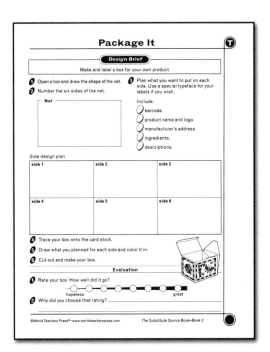

Technology
Package It (page 79)

Students learn how a box is put together using overlaps and the information which must be included on the packaging. They design the cover of a box for a specific product.

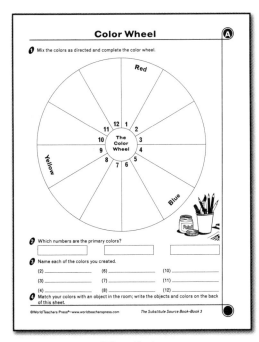

The Arts
Color Wheel (page 83)

Students learn the primary colors and how they combine to make other colors. They use their imagination and knowledge of colors in the natural world to name manufactured colors.

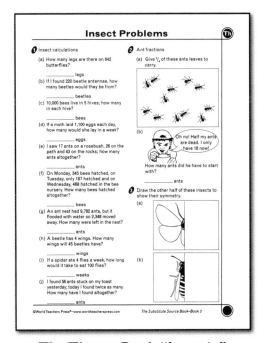

The Theme Pack "Insects"
Insect Problems (page 87)

Students use their knowledge of insect anatomy to calculate math problems. They use mirrors to make accurate symmetrical drawings.

Record of Worksheet Use

The Substitute Source Book (Grades 5–6)

Teacher's Name: _____

	Title of Lesson	School: Class:	Class:	Class:	Class:	Class:	School: Class:	Class:	Class:	Class:	Class:
1.	Book Review										
2.	Informational Text Review										
3.	Program Review Poster										
4.	Early Explorers										
5.	The Old Car										
6.	Early Morning on a Dairy Farm										
7.	Setting Up an Aquarium										
8.	Exploring Ancient Egypt										
9.	Exploring Food										
10.	Ideas for Creative Writing										
11.	Ideas for Informative Writing										
12.	Storywriting Plan										
13.	Direct Speech										
14.	Two-Minute Talks										
15.	School Additions										
16.	Tell Me a Story										
17.	Mental Math										
18.	Number Studies										
19.	Writing Numbers										
20.	Time for Math										
21.	Calendar Activities										

The Substitute Source Book–Book 3   ©World Teachers Press®~www.worldteacherspress.com

Record of Worksheet Use

The Substitute Source Book (Grades 5-6)

Teacher's Name: _____

	Title of Lesson	School:					School:				
		Class:	Class:	Class:	Class:	Class:	Class:	Class:	Class:	Class:	Class:
22.	The Long and Short										
23.	The Shape of Things										
24.	Chances										
25.	Saving Water										
26.	Materials Close Up										
27.	Medicines										
28.	Sun-Safe Poster Plan										
29.	Famous Tower/Bridge Project										
30.	Production Systems										
31.	Explorer Research										
32.	Name Label										
33.	The Kitchen Hand Tool										
34.	Package It										
35.	Clay Monster										
36.	Color Wheel										
37.	Insect Words										
38.	Insect Problems										
39.	Insect Camouflage										
40.	My Life as an Insect										
41.	Insect Observation										
42.	Insect Model										

Class Record Sheet

Teacher's Name: _____

The Substitute Source Book (Grades 5–6)

Title of Lesson	School:						School:					
	Class:	Class:	Class:	Class:			Class:	Class:	Class:	Class:		

Substitute Teacher Survival Kit

Every substitute teacher should have a supply of resources packed and ready to go. These should include:

Resource	Check box
Rewards such as stickers, colored dots, stamps, etc.	
Stories appropriate to each grade/year level; for example, Roald Dahl's *Revolting Rhymes*.	
A collection of **poems**, **singing games** and **songs** for lesson breaks, attention-getting and settling purposes.	
Story tapes/CDs, useful for settling students, to reward students for good behavior (they may serve as page-turners), or to allow the teacher to rest his/her voice or to observe the students.	
Pens and **pencils** for marking work.	
A collection of **"busy-work" sheets**, such as word searches, crosswords, or intricate shape pattern sheets to color for early finishers	
A **name badge**.	
A labeled **mug** for tea or coffee.	
Some **games** to teach the students, such as Hangman.	
A collection of 30 or more interesting **pictures** to use as motivation for storywriting.	

Substitute teachers should keep resources relevant to specific worksheets in a folder or plastic sleeve to enable them to be found easily.

Book Review

| **Learning Area** |
| English |
| **Strands** |
| Reading |
| Writing |
| Speaking and Listening |

Indicators

• Understands the purpose and value of book reviews.

• Writes a review of a familiar story.

Resources

• Short, fictional stories which the students have read and wish to review (class or school library or own copy)

Lesson Plan and Organization

• Discuss the purpose of book reviews and consider how they may affect the choice of books selected for reading.

• Complete a book review of a familiar story with the students to ensure they understand how to complete the sheet.

• Students complete the worksheets individually. (This exercise may also be completed as a homework exercise.)

Additional Activities

• Students present their reviews to the class or a small group.

• Students write or tell the story in their own words.

• Display storybooks and review sheets in the library.

• Students research their chosen author or the chosen book.

Answers

Teacher check

Book Review

1 What is the book title? _____

2 Where does the story take place? (setting)

_____

3 The main characters in the book are: _____

_____

4 About the book: (a) Author: _____

(b) Illustrator: _____

(c) Year of publication: _____

(d) Number of pages: _____

5 Select five interesting words from the book.

6 Write a summary of the book in a few sentences.

_____

_____

_____

_____

_____

_____

_____

7 Draw a picture which illustrates a scene from the story.

8 Give the book a rating from 1 to 5.

hopeless   great!

9 Would you recommend this book to a friend?   ○ yes   ○ no

Why?_____

_____

<table>
<tr><td>

Learning Area

English

Strands

Reading

Writing

Speaking and Listening

</td></tr>
</table>

Indicators

- Understands the difference between fiction and nonfiction.
- Writes a review of an information book.
- Delivers the review to an audience.

Resources

- Sufficient nonfiction texts for each student to read and review (This may also be done with one book shared between two students!)

Web Sites

- Students use the Internet to research the book or an author they have chosen.

Lesson Plan and Organization

- Discuss the layout of nonfiction books. Using examples, show the contents pages, highlighting different topics and sections, the glossary and index. Explain that although a standard pattern is followed, the exact format is dependent on the subject matter and level of understanding of the target audience.
- Discuss the purpose of book reviews and consider how they may affect the choice of books selected for reading.
- Complete a nonfiction book review with students to ensure they understand the specific vocabulary and where to find the information.
- Students complete the worksheets individually.
- Students read their reviews to the class or a small group.

Additional Activities

- Draw or paint a large illustration from the book.
- Design a poster promoting the book or a new book cover.
- Tally the class information from Question 4 and present it using different graphical forms.
- Use the Internet to further research the topic of the book and plan a short project to present to the class.
- Display the books with the reviews, illustrations and promotional posters.

Answers

Teacher check

Informational Text Review

Complete the information.

1 Book title: _____

2 Publisher: _____

3 Book summary (a brief description of the content of the book):

_____

_____

_____

4 Book numbers:

(a) Year of publication _____   (b) Number of chapters _____

(c) Number of pages _____   (d) Book dimensions _____ x _____

5 Three interesting words from the book:

6 Two interesting facts from the book:

• _____

_____

• _____

_____

7 Illustrations:

(a) The illustrations were:

◯ photos

◯ diagrams

◯ cartoons

◯ pictures

(You may need to check more than one box.)

(b) Draw and label an illustration for the book.

Program Review Poster

Learning Area
English
Strands
Viewing
Speaking and Listening

Indicators

• Makes notes on topic while viewing program.

• Plans and designs poster using notes.

Resources

• A half-hour documentary (science or society and environment)

• Poster board, selection of writing materials, crayons and marker pens

• Magazines from which to gather appropriate pictures relevant to the topic (optional)

Lesson Plan and Organization

• Introduce the documentary topic to ascertain what the students already know about the subject.

• Explain how they are to plan and design a poster for the documentary. Use the headings on the student page to provide suggestions. Advise students to make notes during the program.

• After viewing, students work in groups, sharing ideas.

• Students design posters in draft form on a separate sheet of paper.

• Students discuss how their posters might be improved before beginning their final copies on poster board.

• Students create their posters from the available materials.

Additional Activities

• Students give oral presentations advertising the documentary, using the posters as an aid.

• Display the posters in the school library or wherever the documentary may be viewed by others.

Answers

Teacher check

Program Review Poster

Design a poster to advertise a television show.

1 Things to include:

◯ Program title in special typeface.

◯ Illustrations to describe the program.

◯ Interesting vocabulary relating to the topic.

◯ Descriptive sentences/phrases explaining key ideas.

◯ Name of presenter.

◯ Length of program.

◯ Border design.

2 Plan your poster in the space below.

| **Learning Area** |
| English |
| Environment |
| **Strands** |
| Reading |
| Writing |

Indicators

- Uses meaning of text to place correct words in a cloze.
- Learns and defines topic-specific vocabulary.
- Uses resources to access information to answer specific questions.

Resources

- Dictionary
- A collection of library books on several explorers (optional)
- Access to the internet and specific sites for research (optional)

Web Sites

- http://www.cdli.ca/CITE/explorer.htm
- http://www.win.tue.nl/cs/fm/engels/discovery/index.html
- This web site gives the list of explorers from the above site, in alphabetical order.
  http://www.win.tue.nl/cs/fm/engels/discovery/alpha.html

Lesson Plan and Organization

- Discuss why people needed to explore. List reasons on the board. (Other answers may be obtained from the web sites given!)
- Read through the student page before students complete the activities. The answers to Questions 2 and 3 may be discussed using students' own words.

Additional Activities

- Students complete short "explorer" plays/skits, ensuring that the reasons for exploration are given.

- Students plan their explorer research as a mini-topic to present to the class.
- Students complete an explorer research (see pages 72–73 "Explorer Research").
- Students use vocabulary from the books and Web sites to devise "explorer" word search and crossword puzzles, or cloze activities.
- Students prepare a class time line of exploration, with each pair or group adding information about their chosen explorer.
- Draw, paint, or make models of explorer ships. Research the designs and include the main features.
- On a world map, trace the journeys of the explorers, using a different color for each one.

Answers

1. 1. brave 2. ships 3. becoming
   4. new 5. gems 6. foodstuffs
   7. live 8. else 9. war
   10. spread 11. important 12. Explorers
   13. to 14. kings 15. larger

2. (a) explorers (b) inventions (c) brave

3. (a) someone who lives nearby
   (b) a special stone which is cut, polished and used in jewelry
   (c) having great value

Early Explorers

1 Find the correct word from the word bank to complete the text.

Word Bank

to
live
kings
foodstuffs
gems
else
war
larger
becoming
important
new
Explorers
ships
brave
spread

Early explorers were very _____[1] to sail their little wooden _____[2] into unknown parts of the world. They had many reasons for _____[3] explorers.

They sometimes went to find _____[4] things like precious _____[5], gold, _____[6] and wonderful inventions to bring back home. Sometimes they just wanted to _____[7] somewhere _____[8] in the world because they couldn't get along with their neighbors. They needed to escape from _____[9].

Some explorers _____[10] their religious beliefs to other people in the world. They considered it _____[11] to tell others about their God.

_____[12] sometimes sailed _____[13] find new lands for their _____[14] and queens, who wanted to make their countries _____[15] and richer.

2 Find a word from the text to match each meaning.

(a) People who search or travel to discover things.   _____

(b) Things designed for the first time.   _____

(c) Very courageous and daring.   _____

3 Write the dictionary meanings for these words:

(a) neighbor _____

_____

(b) gems _____

(c) precious _____

The Old Car

Learning Area

English

Strands

Reading

Writing

Indicators

• Uses meaning of text to place correct words in a cloze.

• Understands topic-specific vocabulary.

• Writes own conclusion to imaginative text.

Resources

• Dictionary for each student (or pair of students)

Lesson Plan and Organization

• Read the words in the word bank, asking students to define each. Write them on the board.

• Read through the text, asking students to consider which words would best fit in the spaces.

• Discuss what might happen next in the story. Consider humorous and calamitous possibilities.

• Students complete Questions 1 and 2 of the worksheet, ensuring the cloze passage makes sense and the puzzle words are correctly spelled.

• Students complete Question 3.

Additional Activities

• Students read their story endings to the class.

• Students illustrate part of the story, attempting to show the mood of the scene; for example, Mr. Emilio fuming.

• In groups, students choose an ending and act out the whole scene, including an introduction with Tony's assurance that the car is roadworthy. Each group performs its sketch to the class.

• Students write their version of the complete story.

Answers

1.
1. old	2. gravel	3. wheel	4. fuming	5. Motors	6. ready
7. back	8. start	9. key	10. motor	11. hand	12. far

2.

3. Teacher check

The Old Car

1 Find the correct word from the word bank to complete the text.

Word Bank
back
far
fuming
gravel
hand
key
motor
Motors
old
start
ready
wheel

The _____[1] car sat silently on the _____[2] road. Its owner, Mr. Emilio, sat quietly behind the steering _____[3]. His face said it all. He was silently _____[4].

Tony, the mechanic from Walker _____[5], had said, "She's a beauty, Pedro. She's all _____[6] to go. You could drive her to Boston and _____[7]."

But it just wouldn't _____[8]. He turned the _____[9] again. A loud clanking sound came from the _____[10] but there was no sound of an engine turning over. Pedro struck the steering wheel with his _____[11]. He wasn't sure where he was or how _____[12] he would have to walk to get help.

2 Complete this puzzle using words from the word bank.

Across
1. Used to steer a car
3. To get going
4. Very angry
7. Prepared
8. Not new
9. Used to start a car

Down
2. Found on your arm
4. A long way
5. An engine
6. Small stones or pebbles

3 Write what you think happened next in the story.

_____

_____

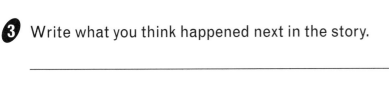

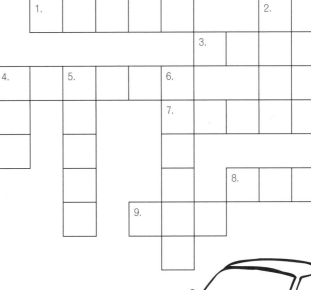

Early Morning on a Dairy Farm

Learning Area

English

Strands

Reading

Writing

Viewing

Indicators

- Extracts specific information from text.

- Interprets text to answer inferential questions.

- Uses own opinion and information from text to provide evaluative answers.

Resources

- Stimulus pictures of cows, dairies, dairy products (optional)

- Some information books on dairying to help with discussion (optional)

- Video/DVD of dairy farming (optional)

Lesson Plan and Organization

- Discuss the reason for rising early. Select students to give oral accounts of having to rise early; for example, to go on vacation, sport training, etc.

- Discuss the task of milking and the equipment required for small and large herds, the range of dairy products available, the role of the cow as a "raw material" in the dairy industry.

- Read the text with the students. Highlight topic and unknown words. Discuss their meanings.

- Students reread the text silently.

- Read through the questions explaining that they may be:
  Literal – requiring a specific literal answer where all information is provided in the text.
  Inferential – requiring the students to infer the answer from partial information provided in the text.
  Evaluative – requiring the students to make a judgment based on information in the text and their own opinion(s).

- Students complete the worksheet independently.

Additional Activities

- Use the topic words for further language activities; e.g., finding definitions, wordbuilding.

- Use the text for language work on punctuation, spelling and grammar.

- Illustrate the text, selecting specific events to sequence in a series of boxes.

- Plan and research a dairying project. Choose from: dairy farming, the dairy industry, dairy products.

- Visit a dairy farm or a dairy product factory.

- Present all work produced in a display about dairying.

Answers

1. spider webs

2. to teach them to drink from a bucket

3. – 6. Teacher check

Early Morning on a Dairy Farm

At 5 a.m. in winter, it is cold and frosty here on the dairy farm.

I rose slowly and pulled on my old clothes and overalls. I was milking that morning as Dad was away. I tiptoed along the veranda so I would not wake Mom. Once outside, I pulled on my rubber boots.

I set off through the back gate, down the dirt track towards the dairy. My warm breath made steam clouds in the cold air. The red glow over the hills to the east heralded the arrival of another dawn. A willy wagtail chattered loudly to let me know I was near its spider-web nest in the pine tree.

Unexpectedly, a soft lowing from the dairy caught my attention. There was a cow already waiting! She must have been the one that gave birth to a heifer the day before and was now looking for her calf. Calves are removed from their mothers the day they are born so they can be taught to drink from a bucket. For a few days, the cows pine for their young.

I opened the dairy yard gate and trudged down the muddy lane towards the cow paddock, warily passing the sad-eyed mother. When I arrived, some of the Friesian cows were already moving up. I moved cautiously around the paddock, calling and whistling. Large forms moved past me in the half-light, but I kept my attention on the hoof holes and drains on the ground. The cold made me shiver, so I lay down for a moment in a warm "cow's nest" in the long grass. This was a welcome winter treat for me. I could still smell the odor of the cow's body, but as it was lovely and snug, I didn't mind at all.

Gradually, all the cows entered the lane. I shut the gate and opened another to the paddock where the cows would spend the day. Then I hurried down the lane after the receding tails of the herd, ready for the task ahead.

1 What do willy wagtails use to make their nests? _____

2 Why are calves taken from their mothers after only one day?

_____

3 Give two clues which show it is early morning.

• _____   • _____

4 Why do you think the person called and whistled as he/she went around the paddock?

_____

5 (a) How old do you think the person is? _____

(b) What clues lead you to believe this? _____

_____

6 How would you feel if you had to do the milking on this farm?

_____

Setting Up an Aquarium

| **Learning Area** |
| English |
| **Strand** |
| Reading |

Indicators

- Interprets text to answer literal, inferential and evaluative questions.
- Uses dictionary skills to find word definitions.
- Demonstrates understanding of text by ordering instructions correctly.

Resources

- Dictionary
- An aquarium for demonstration (optional)
- Information books on tropical fish and how to keep them (optional)

Web Sites

- http://www.thekrib.com
- http://www.tropicalfishcentre.co.uk
- http://badmanstropicalfish.com

Lesson Plan and Organization

- Find out how many students have an aquarium at home. Ask them to present a brief account of their aquariums. Encourage questions from the class.
- Read the text with the students. Highlight topic and unknown words.
- Orally ask general questions about setting up an aquarium. Compare student accounts with the text.
- Students reread the text silently.
- Read through the questions explaining that they may be:
  Literal – requiring a specific literal answer where all information is provided in the text.
  Inferential – requiring the students to infer the answer from the partial information provided in the text.
  Evaluative – requiring the students to make a judgment based on information in the text and their own opinion(s).
- Students complete the worksheet independently.

Additional Activities

- Follow-up discussion using inferential and evaluative questioning. For example, "Why not put the tank in direct sunlight?" or "Where would you put an aquarium in your home. Explain why."
- Using a selection of materials, design and make a model aquarium in the classroom or set up a real one!
- Use information books and the Internet to research material for a project on tropical fish.
- Present all work produced in a tropical fish/aquarium display. Use topic words in the background.
- Rewrite the text as a procedure with a comprehensive list of instructions.
- Use the text for language work on punctuation, spelling and grammar.

Answers

1. & 2.
   Teacher check

3. (a) filter (b) heater (c) light

4. (a) oxygenate – to add oxygen
   (b) filter – to strain a liquid and remove unwanted materials
   (c) flakes – small, thin pieces of a substance

5. 3, 5, 2, 1, 4

Setting Up an Aquarium

When setting up an aquarium, you need to make sure you have all the right equipment. You will need a large glass aquarium, about 3.25 feet long, 12 inches wide, and 16 inches high. This will be big enough for about 15 tropical freshwater fish. You will need a solid stand to put it on, an aquarium light, a water heater, a thermometer, some special gravel for the bottom and a water filter to clean and oxygenate the water. Freshwater fish need oxygen added to the water or they will die. You can buy some large rocks from an aquarium shop. Rocks from the garden may have germs on them. Buy some fish flakes and plant food.

First, clean the tank with fresh water. It is very important that you don't use detergent at all. Now put the clean tank on the stand in a place away from the sun and near a power outlet. Wash the gravel in a bucket under a running hose. The water should overflow the bucket. Stir the gravel with your hand until the water runs clear. This may take some time. Wash the rocks well, too. Now add the clean gravel to the aquarium and spread it along the bottom about $3/_4 - 1$ inch thick. Arrange the rocks where you think they will look good. Fill the tank with water until it is 4 inches from the top. Install the filter by attaching it to the side of the tank. Plug it in and turn it on. Fix the heater in place and turn it on too. Leave the tank running for two days to let it settle and warm up. The water needs to be 78.8° F for the fish to survive.

Buy some water plants from the aquarium store. Add the plants and the right amount of plant food to the aquarium. Install the light, but only turn it on during the day. The next day, add some small, cheap fish to the tank. This will test the tank to see if it is ready for more, larger fish. Feed the fish a little as soon as you put them in the tank and again the next morning. If they survive for a few days, add some larger fish. Don't put all the fish in at once. Only buy two or three at a time. Feed your fish once a day at the same time. Don't give them too much or they will die. They only have tiny tummies to fill! Congratulations, now you have a lovely water feature in your home.

What do you think?

1 Why don't you wash the tank with detergent?

_____

2 Why is it wise to buy only small, cheap fish at first?

_____

3 What three appliances need a power outlet?

• _____ • _____ • _____

4 Find the dictionary meaning of these words.

(a) oxygenate _____

(b) filter _____

(c) flakes _____

5 Number these instructions in the correct order from 1 to 5.

◯ Add plants to the aquarium.

◯ Put some large fish in.

◯ Fill the tank with water.

◯ Wash the gravel in a bucket.

◯ Add small fish to the aquarium.

Exploring Ancient Egypt

Learning Area

English

Strands

Reading

Viewing

Indicators

- Extracts information from a range of sources.
- Uses dictionary skills to find word definitions.
- Demonstrates understanding of topic words by using them in the correct context.

Resources

- Information books, maps, posters and videos/DVDs on Ancient Egypt (optional)
- A dictionary for each student

Web Sites

- Type "Ancient Egypt" into your search engine for a selection of Web sites.
- http://www.ancient-egypt.org
- http://www.ancientegypt.co.uk/menu.html

Lesson Plan and Organization

- *Note:* This lesson may be used as an introduction to Ancient Egypt.
- Look at the list of topic words on the worksheet. Define and discuss any unknown words. Ask students to add two topic words of their own. These may be spelling errors from previous tests or other words relating to the topic.
- Read through the rest of the worksheet to ensure instructions are clear. One section may be corrected at the time it is completed.

Additional Activities

- As a class, plan a topic web for a project on Ancient Egypt. Ensure all main areas are covered. Divide the class into groups and give each one a part of the project to research. Plan a wall display, giving each group space to mount their work.
- Create crosswords and word searches using topic words.

- Design and make models of Ancient Egyptian technology; e.g., pyramid, boat, shadoof, sarcophagus.
- Present all work produced in an Ancient Egypt display. Use topic words in the background.

Answers

1. (a) Nile, Thebes, Cairo
   (b) Nefertiti, Cleopatra
   (c) Horus, Isis, Sphinx

2. (a) & (b) Teacher check

3. (a) embalm – to preserve a body by treating with chemicals
   (b) papyrus – tall plant; material used for writing on
   (c) nobleman – belonging to the ruling class of a country

4. (a) Nefertiti, Cleopatra
   (b) cats, oxen
   (c) Thebes, Cairo (d) Isis, Horus

5.

S	P	H	I	N	X	C	N
I	Y	J	F	Q	M	A	S
P	R	I	E	S	T	T	K
P	A	P	Y	R	U	S	I
E	M	B	A	L	M	G	S
I	I	M	U	M	M	Y	B
X	D	H	O	R	U	S	O
C	A	I	R	O	X	E	N

sphinx
Cairo
Horus
mummy
embalm
papyrus
priest
oxen
cats
pyramid

Exploring Ancient Egypt

Topic Words

- embalm
- mummy
- papyrus
- Nefertiti
- pyramid
- temple
- Horus
- Nile
- Thebes
- Cleopatra
- pharaoh
- Cairo
- Isis
- Sphinx
- oxen
- cats
- priest
- _____
- _____

1 Write each capitalized topic word in the correct box.

Place Names	People Names	Gods and Statues

2 Use these word pairs in a sentence.

(a) oxen, Nile _____

(b) cats, pyramid _____

3 Find the dictionary meanings of these words.

(a) embalm _____

(b) papyrus _____

(c) nobleman _____

4 Using the topic words find two:

(a) pharaohs _____   _____

(b) animals _____   _____

(c) places _____   _____

(d) gods _____   _____

5 In the puzzle, find and write ten topic words from the list.

S	P	H	I	N	X	C	N
I	Y	J	F	Q	M	A	S
P	R	I	E	S	T	T	K
P	A	P	Y	R	U	S	I
E	M	B	A	L	M	G	S
I	I	M	U	M	M	Y	B
X	D	H	O	R	U	S	O
C	A	I	R	O	X	E	N

_____   _____

_____   _____

_____

_____

_____

_____

Exploring Food

Learning Area

English

Strands

Speaking and Listening

Reading

Writing

Indicators

- Extracts information from a list of words.
- Demonstrates understanding of topic words by using them in the correct context.
- Classifies topic words into correct groups.

Resources

- Information books and posters/pictures of food (optional)
- A range of different types of food (These may be obtained from student or own resources.)

Lesson Plan and Organization

- Look at the range of food provided and discuss which food group they belong in. Discuss healthy choices of food.
- Discuss reasons why some foods may be eaten raw while others need to be processed. Our bodies can digest some foods in their raw state—e.g. fruits and most vegetables—while others need to be cooked first, e.g., lentils, split peas, and vegetables such as potato, rutabaga and turnip.
- Explain that some foods need to be preserved to prevent spoilage and increase shelf life; e.g., by freezing, drying and canning. Ask students to give examples of food spoilage (mold on bread, foul smell of fish and eggs).
- Look at the list of topic words on the worksheet. Ask students to orally define each and add two of their own.
- Read through the rest of the worksheet to ensure instructions are clear.
- Students read their answers to Question 4 to the class.

Additional Activities

- Devise taste tests to try on the class.
- Use modeling clay to make fruit and vegetables. Use these to make models of animals; e.g., using "bananas" for tails, "potatoes" for heads, "watermelons" for legs.
- Brainstorm ideas for research; e.g., how certain foods (bread, sausages, flour, molasses) are made. Ask students to present their research as a flow diagram.
- Use pictures of food cut from magazines to categorize into the main food groups.
- Create crosswords and word searches using topic words.
- Prepare a class cookbook. Each student brings in a favorite recipe. Students copy recipes to try at home. If practical, examples may be brought to school to share.

Answers

1. (a) taste (b) chew (c) lunch (d) cheese
2. (a) carrot (b) apple (c) bread (d) steak
3. (a) tastes (b) dinners (c) lunches (d) cheeses
4. (a) – (c) Teacher check
5. (a) breakfast, lunch, dinner, supper
   (b) cereal, meat, vegetable, fruit
   (c) chew, taste
6. (a) – (b) Teacher check

Exploring Food

Topic Words

beans

carrot

vegetable

fruit

meat

cereal

toast

dinner

apple

cheese

supper

chew

taste

lunch

steak

breakfast

milk

bread

_____

_____

1 Choose the correct word from the list to fill in the blanks.

(a) Our nose and tongue help us _____ our food.

(b) We use our teeth to _____ our food.

(c) At school we have to eat our _____.

(d) We make _____ from milk.

2 Match the pairs.

(a) vegetable •   • bread

(b) fruit   •   • steak

(c) toast   •   • carrot

(d) meat   •   • apple

3 Make these words plural.

(a) taste   _____

(b) dinner   _____

(c) lunch   _____

(d) cheese   _____

4 Use these pairs of words in sentences.

(a) fruit, cereal _____

(b) supper, cheese _____

(c) chew, apple _____

5 Write the topic words that go under each heading.

Words That Tell When We Eat	Words That Name Food Groups	Words That Tell What We Do to Food

6 Read and draw.

(a) A basket with six red apples and one carrot.

(b) A plate of steak and vegetables.

Ideas for Creative Writing

Learning Area
English
Strands
Writing
Speaking and Listening

Indicators

- Plans and writes a text of specific length.
- Uses descriptive vocabulary to enhance the quality of writing.
- Proofreads and edits own work.

Resources

- Motivational material to promote creative writing of chosen starter (optional)

Lesson Plan and Organization

- *Note:* This lesson may be divided into individual lessons for use over four days.
- Spend time discussing possible ideas. Write ideas on the board.
- Explain that the time given for writing is limited.
- Discuss the need for descriptive vocabulary, making use of adjectives and adverbs to produce an interesting, exciting piece of prose. Write words on the board.
- Students write their first draft on a separate sheet of paper. When this draft is complete, allow them time to proofread and edit.
- If time allows, students swap work with a partner to look for further edits.
- Students write their work neatly on the lesson sheet.

Additional Activities

- Students read their work to the class or a group.
- Students illustrate their work.
- Discuss "What happened before?" or "What happened next?" to extend the piece of writing.
- Dissect work. How many sentences, adjectives, adverbs, etc.? Collate alternative "said" words from all pieces of work and display in the classroom to promote further use. Study commonly misspelled words.
- Students use different typefaces to print work from a computer. Display with illustration.
- Make class booklets to show the different pieces of writing which have all come from the original starter.
- Students repeat the activity using the following story starters:
  "I saw a tiny flicker …"   "I was at the very top of the tree …"
  "He was halfway down the slide when …"   "One moonlit night …"

Answers

Teacher check

Ideas for Creative Writing

When I opened the front door _____

_____

_____

_____

_____

The old man slowly stood up _____

_____

_____

_____

_____

Hamburgers again! _____

_____

_____

_____

_____

Deep in the forest _____

_____

_____

_____

Ideas for Informative Writing

Learning Area
English

Strands
Writing

Speaking and Listening

Indicators
- Plans and writes a concise summary of a factual topic.
- Recognizes the main points to be included in the summary.
- Proofreads and edits own work.

Resources
- Motivational material to promote informative writing of chosen topic (optional)

Lesson Plan and Organization
- *Note:* This lesson may be divided into individual lessons for use over four days.
- Choose the topic.
- Spend time discussing the main points of the topic. Write points on the board.
- Write a basic plan on the board to guide students in their writing, explaining that the final piece of work will be brief. The text will need to contain the important points of the topic.
- Explain that the time given for writing is limited.
- Discuss the need for accurate, concise language. Only the facts are required. Personal preferences and opinions, in this instance, are inappropriate.
- Students write their first draft on a separate sheet of paper. When this draft is complete, allow them time to proofread and edit.
- If time allows, students swap work with a partner to look for further edits.
- Students write work neatly onto the lesson sheet.

Additional Activities
- Students read their work to the class.
- Students illustrate each paragraph.
- Students develop their paragraphs into a completed project of work.
- Design a topic web to include all the areas that could be researched. In small groups, students research one area of the topic web, presenting it as uniquely as possible.
- Students compile a list of six questions, the answers to which are found in their research. After all groups have delivered their research, the whole class takes part in a quiz. Students are not allowed to answer their own questions!
- Make class booklets of the completed topic.

Answers
Teacher check

Ideas for Informative Writing

Dinosaurs

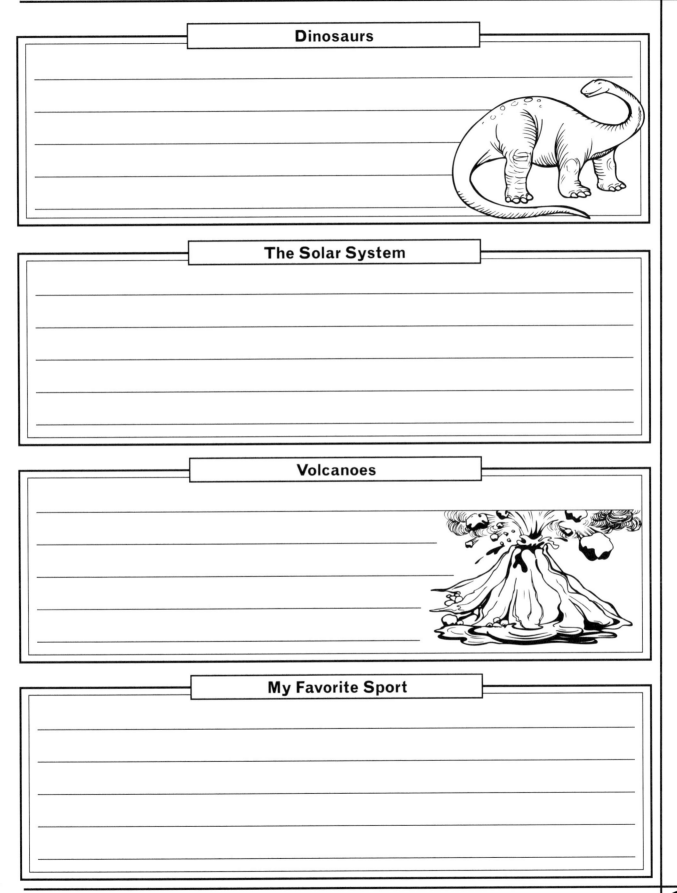

The Solar System

Volcanoes

My Favorite Sport

The Substitute Source Book–Book 3

Storywriting Plan

<table>
<tr><td>

Learning Area

English

Strands

Writing

Speaking and Listening

</td><td>

Indicators

- Uses a plan to organize ideas for a story.
- Understands the "beginning," "middle" and "end" structure of a story.
- Makes notes in preparation for writing.

</td></tr>
</table>

Resources

- Motivational material to promote ideas for storywriting (optional)
- Computer access for publishing (optional)

Lesson Plan and Organization

- Choose the topic.
- Explain and discuss the "dot point" rules for planning.
  "Dot point" rules:
  (i) Write only one idea or event per point.
  (ii) Write a word or phrase only (no sentences).
- Explain and discuss how a story structure follows the plan on the sheet, and the prompting questions in each section guide the author's writing.
- Students make a draft of their plan before writing it on the "storywriting plan" sheet. The final story, written from the plan, may differ from their original ideas. This gives them the opportunity to proofread and edit their work.
- Students write their final ideas on the writing plan and give the story a title.
- From the writing plan, students write the complete story. It may be preferable to do this after a break, giving students time to refresh and tackle the final stage with more inspiration.
- Students select a title for their story.
- Students may wish to read their stories to the class.

Additional Activities

- Students illustrate a scene or character from their story.
- Students type stories into the computer and publish an illustrated class storybook which they can read to students in another class.
- Have a competition to design a cover for the class book.
- Display plans and final copies together on a wall with the illustrations.

Answers

Teacher check

Storywriting Plan

Title

Beginning

Who is in it?

Where and when is the story taking place?

What's going to happen?

Middle

What problems do the characters face?

How and why are things happening?

Draw your main character

Ending

How is the problem solved?

What happens to finish the story?

What do the characters think at the end?

Draw some action from your story

Direct Speech

Learning Area

English

Strands

Writing

Speaking and Listening

Indicators

- Uses quotation marks appropriately.
- Chooses vocabulary which best describes the scene of a cartoon.
- Uses vocabulary to accurately illustrate a joke.

Resources

- A selection of cartoons requiring an introductory sentence plus a two-person exchange (optional)

Lesson Plan and Organization

- Share the cartoon jokes on the sheet with the students and discuss what is happening in them. Explain that an introductory sentence sets the scene, then each character has a turn to speak.

- Students complete Question 1 on the worksheet.

- Explain the rules for writing direct speech before asking students to complete part 2, using the format of Question 1 as a guide.

Additional Activities

- Students write and illustrate jokes and cartoons of their own and then join them to form a class joke book.

- In pairs, students act out jokes for the class.

Answers

Teacher check

Direct Speech

1 Draw the cartoon for this joke.

> A man sat sadly in the doctor's room with a bandage over his eye.
>
> The man said, "Doctor, whenever I drink a cup of tea I get this sharp pain in my eye!"
>
> The doctor replied, "You know, you should remove the teaspoon from your cup before you drink the tea."

2 In sentences, write these cartoons as jokes. Explain what is happening and use quotation marks for each character's speech.

(a)

_____

_____

_____

_____

_____

_____

_____

_____

_____

(b)

_____

_____

_____

_____

_____

_____

_____

Two-Minute Talks

Learning Area

English

Strands

Writing

Speaking and Listening

Indicators

- Relates a known procedure or event in logical sequence.
- Sustains a conversation on a familiar topic.
- Demonstrates an emerging awareness of strategies for different types of interaction.

Resources

- Objects for talks
- Stopwatch

Topic Ideas

- Games I Like
- A Good Holiday
- Sports Stars
- Playtime
- Television
- My Pet
- Dogs and Cats
- Something I Saw
- A Strange Animal

Lesson Plan and Organization

- This lesson may be introduced a few days in advance to give students time to choose a topic and collect their resources. Students may choose their own topics or choose from the list above.
- Divide the class into groups of four or five students and provide each group with a planning sheet. Explain the use of "dot points" (one idea per point, words or phrases only) in the planning notes section.
- Students consider their topic choices and write about four or five dot points to cover the main ideas. These are then ranked in a logical order. Resources to enhance delivery of the talk are listed, plus any further notes to be mentioned. The topic should take no longer than two minutes.
- The stopwatch is set by the teacher.
- The self-evaluation section of the sheet should be discussed before the students have given their talks to give them suggestions for good delivery and to explain the importance of keeping to the plan.
- Students may be given time to practice their talks at home or at recess before presenting them to the group, as well as time to collect any relevant aids.
- When rating their performance, students must try to be objective. It may help if, within their groups, they also evaluate each other and offer comments on how well objectives have been met. This should be done after each individual talk to prevent confusion.
- Students give their talks and complete their worksheets.

Additional Activities

- Talks could be videorecorded or audiotaped and played back to the students.
- Talks could be extended and presented in booklet form as mini-topics, with relevant illustrations.
- Students could work out how long it would take for the whole class to present their talks.
- Students may present their talks to another class.
- Illustrate the information presented in the talk and display with resources.

Answers

Teacher check

The Substitute Source Book–Book 3   ©World Teachers Press®~www.worldteacherspress.com

Two-Minute Talks

Planning Sheet

1 My topic: _____

2 Planning notes: (use dot points)

_____

_____

_____

_____

_____

_____

3 Rank your ideas.

4 Aids: _____

5 Notes: _____

Self-Evaluation

How did your talk go?

1 My topic: _____

2 Did you use only the ideas you planned when you gave your talk? ◯ yes ◯ no

3 Comment on how well you achieved these objectives.

   (a) Kept to the time limit _____

   (b) Used eye contact with the group _____

   (c) Spoke clearly _____

   (d) Was polite _____

   (e) Used aids _____

   (f) Followed my plan _____

4 (a) Rate how well you think the talk went.

   hopeless ●——●——●——●——●——● great

   (b) Why did you give this rating? _____

School Additions

Learning Area	**Indicators**

Learning Area

English

Strands

Writing

Speaking and Listening

Indicators

- Looks at an issue objectively.
- Understands the concept of democracy.
- Accepts a democratic decision.

Resources

- Pictures or photos of how different proposed additions may look; e.g., swimming pool, theater (optional)

Lesson Plan and Organization

- Students are to have a small group debate, considering the advantages and disadvantages of a proposed school addition. Explain that a debate is a discussion based on reasoned arguments for and against a proposal. Initially, they work in groups to discuss the proposition and make a final group decision. Each group puts forward reasons for its decision. When all groups have been heard, the final decision is made.

- Decide which addition is to be the subject for debate. Take the class and walk around the area in question.

- Individually, students write a list of "for" and "against" arguments. They then write three of each on the worksheet, making notes on each.

- Divide the students into groups of four to discuss the proposal and give their arguments for and against. As a group, they must make the decision to pass the proposal or not.

- The groups come together as a class to give their arguments and decisions. A "for and against" tally is recorded and the final decision is made.

- Students complete the evaluation section of the sheet. Determine how the decision would have gone if it was to be based on individual votes. Does it differ from the group result?

Additional Activities

- Have a drawing competition to design the new addition.

- Write stories about using the new addition.

- Take photographs of the students working in their groups and display them with the worksheets and final decision tally record.

- Illustrate the information presented in the talk and display with resources.

- Discuss the meaning of democracy, explaining that everyone has the right to an opinion, but decisions are made based on the wishes of the majority. Use examples familiar to the students to explain that democratic decisions which affect them are being made all the time. (What shall we have for dinner? Where shall we go for a picnic? Which game shall we play?)

Answers

Teacher check

School Additions

Suggested school addition: [   ]

1 List three reasons why this would be a good idea. Include notes.

Reasons For		
1.	2.	3.
notes:	notes:	notes:

2 List three reasons why this would be a bad idea. Include notes.

Reasons Against		
1.	2.	3.
notes:	notes:	notes:

How Did It Go?

1 How good were your ideas? _____

2 Comment on how well you achieved these objectives.

(a) Used eye contact with the group _____

(b) Spoke clearly _____

(c) Was polite _____

3 (a) Rate how well you think your arguments went.

hopeless ○—○—○—○——○—○—○—○ great

(b) Why did you give this rating? _____

_____

4 What do you think now? Are you in favor of the addition? Have you changed your mind?

_____

5 What was the overall class decision? ○ for ○ against

Tell Me a Story

| **Learning Area** |
| English |
| **Strands** |
| Writing |
| Speaking and Listening |

Indicators
- Prepares a story plan.
- Considers ways to enhance storytelling.
- Evaluates own storytelling.

Resources
- Lists of suggested topics, characters and plots for storytelling

Web Sites
- The art of storytelling:
  http://www.eldrbarry.net
- About storytelling:
  http://www.nelh.nhs.uk/knowledge_management/km2/storytelling_toolkit.asp

Lesson Plan and Organization
- Tell the class a story.
- Discuss the strategies you employed to capture and hold their interest; e.g., vocal and facial expression, body language.
- Explain the difference between reading and telling a story.
  - For the audience, reading is primarily an aural experience. The expressions, volume and tone of the reader's voice as he/she reads words on a page determine how much a story is enjoyed.
  - The telling of a story is much more visual, similar to the performing of a play. Added to the techniques of reading are the expressions of body language and the use of props.
- Explain that a story has:
  - A beginning, in which the scene is set, introducing the main characters, the location and time.
  - A middle, which includes the main focus and action of the story.
  - An end, in which all things come together and the unraveling of the plot occurs.

- The students are to prepare the plan of a story. Choose a topic and discuss possible characters and plots. Write some suggestions on the board.
- In groups, students discuss ideas and characters, then write their plans on the worksheets. As they do, suggest they imagine themselves telling the story. What expressions will they use? What tone and volume of voice? Students should realize how important the opening sentence is.

Note: The purpose of the students writing main ideas rather than full sentences in the plan is for them to be used as prompts for story telling. This removes the risk of students falling into reading mode.

- When ready, students tell their stories within their groups or, if they wish, to the whole class. Before they do so, explain the purpose of the self-evaluation and the importance of being objective. If appropriate, students could evaluate the performances of other group members.
- Students may retell their story with modifications.

Additional Activities
- Students illustrate stories on large sheets of paper.
- Write the stories in play form, including stage directions; e.g., walking slowly, shouting loudly.

Answers
Teacher check

Tell Me a Story

My story title: _____

Main character: _____

Setting: _____

Opening sentence: _____

_____

Other characters: _____

Story line (main ideas only, not sentences):

Storytelling Tips

- Include who, when and where at the start.
- Use lots of details explaining things.
- Have a climax to the story.
- Use hand gestures and expressions.
- Speak loudly and clearly, look the audience in the eye.

Beginning	Middle	End

Self-Evaluation

My story title: _____

1 Did you keep to the story line you planned when you told the story? ◯ yes ◯ no

Explain what happened. _____

_____

2 Did you ...

(a) use lots of details when you explained things? ◯ none ◯ some ◯ lots

(b) have a climax to your story? ◯ yes ◯ no

(c) use lots of hand gestures and expressions? ◯ none ◯ some ◯ lots

(d) speak clearly and loudly? ◯ never ◯ usually ◯ always

3 (a) Rate your storytelling.

◯—◯—◯—◯—◯—◯—◯—◯
hopeless   great

(b) Why did you give it that rating? _____

_____

Mental Math

Learning Area	**Indicators**

Learning Area

Mathematics

Strands

Number

Indicators
- Solves mental arithmetic problems using the four operations.
- Uses learned strategies to perform mental arithmetic more efficiently.
- Chooses the correct operation to solve number problems.

Resources
- Concrete materials to demonstrate problems (optional)
- Stopwatches (optional)

Lesson Plan and Organization
- Using stopwatches, students time themselves as they complete Sets 1 and 2 and record the result.
- Students mark their own work or swap with a partner as teacher or students give the answers for both sets.
- Before students begin Set 3, work through similar examples using concrete materials to demonstrate the problems. Ask students which number operations are required and work out the answers.
- Students complete Set 3. Those experiencing difficulty may use a calculator. Work through the method of solving each problem.

Additional Activities
- Students make up an oral story to represent a math problem for the class to solve.
- Students create some problems using concrete materials.

Answers
- Set 1
  (a) 25   (b) 4   (c) 11   (d) 6   (e) 12   (f) 30   (g) 3   (h) 9   (i) 11   (j) 6   (k) 4   (l) 7   (m) 11 (n) 11
  (o) 5   (p) 4   (q) 5   (r) 5   (s) 18   (t) 24   (u) 8   (v) 9   (w) 4   (x) 6   (y) 35
- Set 2
  (a) 24   (b) 2   (c) 12   (d) 3   (e) 8   (f) 18   (g) 8   (h) 3   (i) 8   (j) 11   (k) 9   (l) 9   (m) 12 (n) 35
  (o) 20   (p) 5   (q) 4   (r) 8   (s) 5   (t) 6   (u) 28   (v) 6   (w) 14   (x) 7   (y) 12
- Set 3
  (a) $1.5 \times 4 \, kg = 6 \, kg$ (b) $\$5 - \$2.30 = \$2.70$ (c) $12 + 6 = 18$ eggs   (d) $450 - 230 = 220$ girls
  (e) $120 \times 4 = 480$; $^3/_4 = 360$ students   (f) $\$5.40 + \$3 + \$1.80 = \$10.20$
  (g) $\$60 \times 6 = \$360$ (h) $\$2.40 \times 2 = \$4.80$, $\$10 - \$4.80 = \$5.20$ (i) $68 - 55 = 13$ years
  (j) 3 gallons x 4 cartons(quarts)/gallon = 12 cartons

Mental Math

Set 1	Set 2	Set 3

Set 1

(a) 5 x 5 = _____

(b) 16 ÷ 4 = _____

(c) 3 + 8 = _____

(d) 15 − 9 = _____

(e) 4 x 3 = _____

(f) 6 x 5 = _____

(g) 8 − 5 = _____

(h) 16 − 7 = _____

(i) 15 − 4 = _____

(j) 8 − 2 = _____

(k) 12 ÷ 3 = _____

(l) 21 ÷ 3 = _____

(m) 18 − 7 = _____

(n) 3 + 8 = _____

(o) 0 + 5 = _____

(p) 14 − 10 = _____

(q) 12 − 7 = _____

(r) 25 ÷ 5 = _____

(s) 9 x 2 = _____

(t) 3 x 8 = _____

(u) 17 − 9 = _____

(v) 18 ÷ 2 = _____

(w) 12 ÷ 3 = _____

(x) 30 ÷ 5 = _____

(y) 7 x 5 = _____

total: _____ /25

time taken: _____

Set 2

(a) 6 x 4 = _____

(b) 8 ÷ 4 = _____

(c) 5 + 7 = _____

(d) 12 − 9 = _____

(e) 16 ÷ 2 = _____

(f) 9 + 9 = _____

(g) 32 ÷ 4 = _____

(h) 9 ÷ 3 = _____

(i) 24 ÷ 3 = _____

(j) 6 + 5 = _____

(k) 12 − 3 = _____

(l) 16 − 7 = _____

(m) 6 x 2 = _____

(n) 7 x 5 = _____

(o) 5 x 4 = _____

(p) 12 − 7 = _____

(q) 9 − 5 = _____

(r) 11 − 3 = _____

(s) 15 ÷ 3 = _____

(t) 18 ÷ 3 = _____

(u) 7 x 4 = _____

(v) 12 ÷ 2 = _____

(w) 8 + 6 = _____

(x) 7 − 0 = _____

(y) 7 + 5 = _____

total: _____ /25

time taken: _____

Set 3

(a) If a bag of flour weighs 3.3 lb, how much will 4 bags weigh?

_____ lb

(b) If you bought a pie for $2.30, how much change would you get from $5.00?

$_____

(c) How many eggs are there in one and a half dozen?

_____ eggs

(d) There are 450 students at our school. If 230 are boys, how many girls are there?

_____ girls

(e) A quarter of the students at a school went to a concert. If 120 students went, how many didn't go?

_____ students

(f) I paid $5.40 for lunch, $3.00 for bus fare and $1.80 for an ice cream cone. How much did I spend altogether?

$_____

(g) A plumber charges $60 an hour. How much will he earn if he works for 6 hours?

$_____

(h) How much change would I get from $10 if I bought 4.4 lb of sausages at $2.40/lb?

$_____

(i) A boy is 55 years younger than his grandfather. If his grandfather is 68, how old is the boy?

_____ years

(j) How many quart cartons of milk make 3 gallons?

_____ cartons

Number Studies

<table>
<tr><td colspan="2">

Learning Area

Mathematics

Strands

Number

</td><td>

Indicators

- Demonstrates knowledge of place value.
- Demonstrates understanding of the concept of operations.
- Chooses correct operation to solve number problems.
- Demonstrates knowledge of fractions.

</td></tr>
</table>

Resources

- Concrete materials to use in word problems (optional)
- Fraction chart or wheel (optional)
- Similar examples of each question to work through on board (optional)

Lesson Plan and Organization

- Before asking students to complete the worksheet, work through the examples on the board, explaining terminology; i.e., number sentences, word sentences.
- Discuss the fraction chart or wheel (if used).
- Students complete the worksheets.
- Students mark their own work or swap with a partner as teacher works through each question with class.

Additional Activities

- Students use number problems to write a story in words or as a cartoon.
- Students devise a worksheet of problems following the same format. These could be used as a class resource.
- Students make a "match the number sentence with the problem" game. On separate cards, write about eight problems and their corresponding number sentences. Shuffle the cards and time how long it takes to match them. To make it more difficult, add a given number of "rogue" cards which will be left after the others have been matched.

Answers

1. (a) 3,572   (b) 5,319   (c) 4,160   (d) 8,023

2. (a) $12 - 7 \times 5 = 25$ (b) $14 = 7 + 15 - 8$ (c) $3 \times 4 + 6 = 18$ (d) $34 = 6 + 1 \times 12 - 50$
   (e) $5 \times 5 - 6 = 19$ (f) $6 = 3 \times 5 - 9$

3. (a) one thousand fifty-nine   (b) five thousand, four hundred five
   (c) nine thousand, one hundred ten

4. (a) $\$20 - \$8 = \$12$ (b) $18 - 7 = 11$ (c) $30 - 14 = 16$ (d) $25 - 13 = 12$

5. (a) $^3/_4$ (b) $^1/_3$ (c) $^1/_4$

6. (a)   (b)   (c)

The Substitute Source Book–Book 3   ©World Teachers Press®~www.worldteacherspress.com

Number Studies

1 Write the numeral for:

(a) 3 thousands + 5 hundreds + 7 tens + 2 ones _____

(b) 5 thousands + 3 hundreds + 1 ten + 9 ones _____

(c) 6 tens + 4 thousands + 1 hundred _____

(d) 3 ones + 8 thousands + 0 hundreds + 2 tens _____

2 Use x, + or − to make each number sentence true.

(a) 12 ☐ 7 ☐ 5 = 25   (b) 14 = 7 ☐ 15 ☐ 8

(c) 3 ☐ 4 ☐ 6 = 18   (d) 34 = 6 ☐ 1 ☐ 12 ☐ 50

(e) 5 ☐ 5 ☐ 6 = 19   (f) 6 = 3 ☐ 5 ☐ 9

3 Write these numbers out in word form.

(a) 1,059 _____

(b) 5,405 _____

(c) 9,110 _____

4 Write number sentences to solve these problems.

(a) Ryan had $20. He spent $8 on a toy. How much did he have left?

☐ ☐ ☐ = ☐

(b) Jason had 18 marbles in his pocket. He lost 7 on his way home. How many did he have left?

☐ ☐ ☐ = ☐

(c) Emily had 30 colored pens. At the end of the year she had only 14. How many were lost?

☐ ☐ ☐ = ☐

(d) Jade picked a bunch of 25 flowers. In a day 13 had died. How many were still alive?

☐ ☐ ☐ = ☐

5 Write the fraction that represents the shaded part of each shape.

(a)   (b)   (c)

6 Color parts of the shape to match the fraction.

(a) $\frac{2}{3}$ (b) $\frac{1}{4}$ (c) $\frac{3}{5}$

Writing Numbers

Learning Area	**Indicators**
Mathematics	• Demonstrates knowledge of place value.
	• Understands how the addition or subtraction of one factor affects the whole number.
Strands	• Correctly rounds each number to the nearest factor.
Number	

Resources

• Base Ten blocks (optional)

• Examples similar to those in Question 2

Lesson Plan and Organization

• Using resources, work through examples similar to those in Question 1. Also include some examples working backwards; orally give the students the words. Include zero in some examples to help students appreciate that it is vital even though it has no numeric value.

• Work through examples similar to those in Question 2. Demonstrate with Base Ten blocks (if used) so that students can clearly see and understand what occurs when 1, 10 and 100 are added or subtracted.

• Demonstrate examples similar to those in Question 3 . Explain how the "nearest …" is established using the halfway or above rule.

• Students complete the worksheets.

• Students mark their own work or swap with a partner as teacher works through each question with them.

Additional Activities

• Play "Take-a-Cube" and "Build-a-Cube" with Base Ten blocks.

Take-a-Cube – Each student starts with a 1000 cube and throws two dice to make the biggest number to take away from 1000 using the blocks. The first to zero wins.

Build-a-Cube – Students build a thousand cube.

• In pairs, students make up examples of each question type for each other to solve.

Answers

1. (a) 5 hundreds, 2 tens, 6 ones; 526; five hundred twenty six

   (b) 2 thousands, 5 hundreds, 7 tens, 7 ones; 2,577; two thousand, five hundred seventy-seven

2. (a)

1 more	10 more	100 more
200	209	299
199	**199**	**199**
198	189	99
1 less	10 less	100 less

(b)

1 more	10 more	1,000 more
2,200	2,209	3,199
2199	**2,199**	**2,199**
2,198	2,189	1,199
1 less	10 less	1,000 less

3. (a) **9,107**: 9,110; 9,100; 9,000; 10,000   (b) **71,778**: 71,780; 71,800; 72,000; 70,000

   (c) **37,524**: 37,520; 37,500; 38,000; 40,000

Writing Numbers

1 Write down how many thousands, hundreds, tens and ones there are. Write each as a number, then in words.

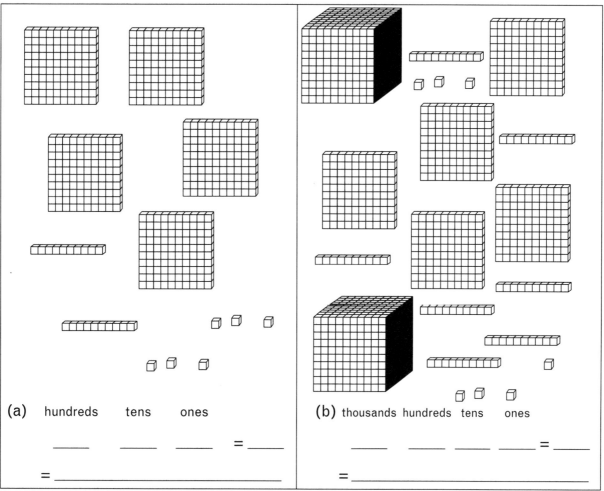

(a) hundreds   tens   ones

_____   _____   _____   = _____

= _____

(b) thousands hundreds tens   ones

_____   _____   _____   _____   = _____

= _____

2 Fill in the table.

(a)

1 more	10 more	100 more
199	**199**	**199**
1 less	10 less	100 less

(b)

1 more	10 more	1,000 more
2,199	**2,199**	**2,199**
1 less	10 less	1,000 less

3 Round each number to the nearest 10, 100, 1,000 and 10,000.

		nearest 10	nearest 100	nearest 1,000	nearest 10,000
(a)	9,107				
(b)	71,778				
(c)	37,524				

Time for Math

Learning Area

Mathematics

Strands

Space and Measurement

Indicators

- Tells the time using both analog and digital clocks.
- Understands that the relationship between the area and perimeter of a shape is not constant.
- Completes information about 3-D shapes.

Resources

- Analog and digital clocks (optional)
- Selection of 3-D shapes

Lesson Plan and Organization

- Demonstrate the different ways of saying the same time; e.g. 3:50 and ten to 4.
- Students complete Questions 1 and 2 on the worksheet.
- Explain definitions of area and perimeter.
- Ask students to complete Question 3 on the worksheet. At least one edge of each square must be touching another. Before they complete part (d), discuss what they have discovered.
- Show students a collection of 3-D shapes. Name them orally. Explain the meanings of face, edge and vertex.
- Students complete Question 4.
- Students tally the number of faces and edges of each shape and collate the tallies on the back of the worksheet. Look for a pattern in the tallies and graph the result.

Additional Activities

- On graph paper, students draw animals, robots, aliens, people, etc. They color and record the total area and perimeter of each figure. Record the area covered by each color.
- Students build constructions using solid shapes.
- Play the solid shape "What Am I?" game; e.g., I have 5 faces, 8 edges and 5 vertices, "What Am I?" Students could include other facts such as the length of the sides. This can be played orally or students could build up a booklet to include all the shapes.

Answers

1. Teacher check
2. Teacher check
3. Teacher check
4. (a) cylinder, 3 faces, 2 edges, 0 vertexes
   (b) triangular pyramid, 4 faces, 6 edges, 4 vertexes
   (c) rectangular prism, 6 faces, 12 edges, 8 vertexes

Time for Math

1 Draw the hands on the clocks to show the time.

(a)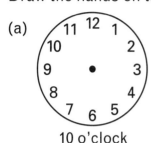
10 o'clock

(b)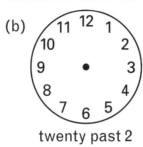
twenty past 2

(c)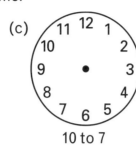
10 to 7

(d)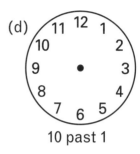
10 past 1

2 Write the time on the digital clocks.

(a)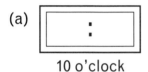
10 o'clock

(b)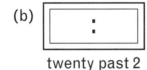
twenty past 2

(c)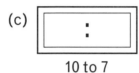
10 to 7

(d)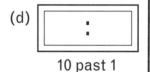
10 past 1

3 (a) Draw a shape with an area of 8 squares.

(b) Draw a different shape using 8 squares.

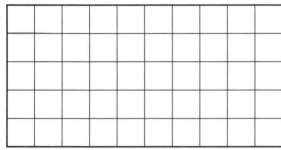
shape 1 = 8 squares

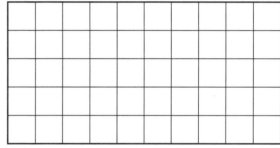
shape 2 = 8 squares

(c) In the spaces below, write the perimeter of each shape.

perimeter = _____ units

perimeter = _____ units

(d) Write a sentence telling about the two perimeters.

_____

_____

4 Use the words below to complete information about the 3-D shapes.

triangular pyramid	rectangular prism	cylinder

(a) Name: _____

_____

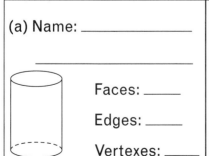

Faces: _____

Edges: _____

Vertexes: _____

(b) Name: _____

_____

Faces: _____

Edges: _____

Vertexes: _____

(c) Name: _____

_____

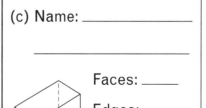

Faces: _____

Edges: _____

Vertexes: _____

Calendar Activities

Learning Area

Mathematics

Strands

Measurement

Indicators

• Uses a calendar to solve problems.

• Learns information about the calendar.

Resources

• Class calendar (optional)

Web Sites

• History of the Calendar:
http://www.infoplease.com/ipa/A0002061.html

• What Happened on This Day?
http://www.scopesys.com/anyday
http://www.historychannel.com/tdih/tdih.
jsp?category=leadstory

Lesson Plan and Organization

• Students indicate when their birthdays occur either by using a class calendar or simply by raising hands as the months of the year are said.

• Give students the opportunity to research events which occurred throughout history on their birth dates (see Web sites).

• As a class, complete Question 1. Mark and discuss.

• Working in small groups, students complete Question 2. Discuss methods of making the calculations easier; e.g., working on months/weeks rather than counting days.

• Students complete the crossword in Question 3 using the Web sites for research if necessary. Students will need to refer to the link "August – History of the Month's Origin" to find the answers to 7 across and 4 down, unless they already know the answer.

Additional Activities

• Students research the history of the calendar (see Web sites) or alternative calendar designs and choose one to make.

• As a class, discuss special days in the school year, including birthdays, and mark on the class calendar.

• Students make a whole-class display of their birthdays using photographs of each student with a line to the appropriate month of the calendar.

• Students begin a "current affairs" diary, recording important local, national and international news. Students take turns at having the responsibility to record this information each day. Name the book "On This Day."

Answers

1. (a) September 9   (b) 31
   (c) 4   (d) Wednesday

2. Teacher check

3.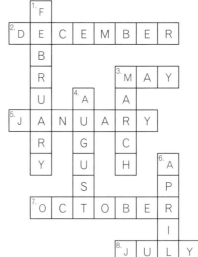

Calendar Activities

S	M	T	W	T	F	S
			January			
1	2	3	4	5	6	7
8	9	10	11	12	13	14
15	16	17	18	19	20	21
22	23	24	25	26	27	28
29	30	31				

S	M	T	W	T	F	S
			February			
				1	2	3
5	6	7	8	9	10	11
12	13	14	15	16	17	18
19	20	21	22	23	24	25
26	27	28				

S	M	T	W	T	F	S
			March			
			1	2	3	4
5	6	7	8	9	10	11
12	13	14	15	16	17	18
19	20	21	22	23	24	25
26	27	28	29	30	31	

S	M	T	W	T	F	S
			April			
30						1
2	3	4	5	6	7	8
9	10	11	12	13	14	15
16	17	18	19	20	21	22
23	24	25	26	27	28	29

S	M	T	W	T	F	S
			May			
	1	2	3	4	5	6
7	8	9	10	11	12	13
14	15	16	17	18	19	20
21	22	23	24	25	26	27
28	29	30	31			

S	M	T	W	T	F	S
			June			
				1	2	3
4	5	6	7	8	9	10
11	12	13	14	15	16	17
18	19	20	21	22	23	24
25	26	27	28	29	30	

S	M	T	W	T	F	S
			July			
30	31					1
2	3	4	5	6	7	8
9	10	11	12	13	14	15
16	17	18	19	20	21	22
23	24	25	26	27	28	29

S	M	T	W	T	F	S
			August			
		1	2	3	4	5
6	7	8	9	10	11	12
13	14	15	16	17	18	19
20	21	22	23	24	25	26
27	28	29	30	31		

S	M	T	W	T	F	S
			September			
					1	2
3	4	5	6	7	8	9
10	11	12	13	14	15	16
17	18	19	20	21	22	23
24	25	26	27	28	29	30

S	M	T	W	T	F	S
			October			
1	2	3	4	5	6	7
8	9	10	11	12	13	14
15	16	17	18	19	20	21
22	23	24	25	26	27	28
29	30	31				

S	M	T	W	T	F	S
			November			
			1	2	3	4
5	6	7	8	9	10	11
12	13	14	15	16	17	18
19	20	21	22	23	24	25
26	27	28	29	30		

S	M	T	W	T	F	S
			December			
31					1	2
3	4	5	6	7	8	9
10	11	12	13	14	15	16
17	18	19	20	21	22	23
24	25	26	27	28	29	30

1 Use the calendar to solve these problems.

(a) What is the date eight weeks from July 15? _____

(b) How many days are there in August? _____

(c) How many Wednesdays are there in June? _____

(d) On which day of the week is May 17? _____

2 Locate the birthdays of three friends and circle them in red.

3 Complete the crossword.

Across

2. The last month

3. Rhymes with hay

5. The first month

7. The eighth month in the old Roman calendar

8. The seventh month

Down

1. The shortest month

3. Rhymes with starch

4. This month was named after the Roman Emperor, Augustus Caesar

6. The fourth month

The Long and Short

Learning Area	**Indicators**
Mathematics	• Suggests realistic estimates of lengths of objects.
Strand	• Measures the length of an object to nearest inch.
Number	

Resources

- Items for students to measure
- Rulers or tape measures marked in inches
- Graph paper

Lesson Plan and Organization

- Discuss the size of item the students would measure in inches. Highlight ridiculous choices such as the running track. Discuss the alternative measures that would be used for these examples; i.e., feet and yards.

- Students choose four items and estimate, measure and calculate the difference before going on to the next. Students measure to the nearest inch above or below. With each item, their estimations should become more accurate.

- Explain that the difference between estimate and measurement indicates accuracy. If the difference is small, the estimate was good because they were close to the real measurement. Their accuracy score is the total of the differences for each item.

- Compare accuracy scores within the class.

- Students use graph paper to indicate estimates and actual measurements using one color for all estimates and another for actual measurements.

Additional Activities

- Students write a report on the activity.
- Take photographs of students measuring and display with written reports.
- From magazines, group pictures into those that would be measured in yards, feet and inches. Display as a montage.

Answers

Teacher check

The Long and Short

1 Select four items you can measure the length of to the nearest inch.
  (a) Draw and label each item.
  (b) Estimate the length of each item, then measure it to the nearest inch.
  (c) Find the difference between your estimate and the actual measurement.

Item 1

Name: _____

Estimate	Measurement	Difference

Item 2

Name: _____

Estimate	Measurement	Difference

Item 3

Name: _____

Estimate	Measurement	Difference

Item 4

Name: _____

Estimate	Measurement	Difference

2 How accurate were your estimates? _____

_____

3 (a) Add the differences for the four items. _____

  (b) What is your accuracy score? [＿＿＿]

  (c) Is a high score better than a low score? ◯ yes ◯ no

  Why? _____

Learning Area

Mathematics

Strand

Space

Indicators

- Understands the meaning of congruency.
- Correctly names 3-D shapes.
- Recognizes the nets of 3-D shapes.

Resources

- Tracing paper
- Collection of 3-D shapes
- Prepared nets of various shapes from the worksheet

Web sites

- See how nets unfold:

  http://www.mathsnet.net/geometry/solid/nets.html

- Making nets:

  http://argyll.epsb.ca/jreed/math8/strand3/3102.htm

Lesson Plan and Organization

- Introduce the concept of congruency and use examples in the classroom.
- Ask students to complete Question 1. Offer suggestions for quickly disregarding some of the options.
- Show the shapes and ask students to name them. Match the concrete shapes to the drawings on the worksheet. Discuss the difference between the 3-D shapes:
  – Pyramid – a solid shape with sides rising to a point.
  – Prism – a solid shape whose ends are any congruent polygon and whose sides are parallelograms.
- Students complete Question 2.

- Introduce the concept of "nets" and ask students to attempt Question 3. To guide them, show them how to determine the number of faces of 3-D shapes. Provide spare paper for them to make the nets.
- Students draw the net for the square pyramid in Question 4.

Additional Activities

- Students make a variety of nets to decorate and display mounted on card stock.
- Students use nets to make boxes for different things.
- Research the nets for different shapes. Display by gluing one face to the backing board, allowing students to fold the sides together to make the shape, so that the "net" and shape are together.

Answers

1. (c) & (m), (e) & (i)
2. (a) square pyramid   (b) cube
   (c) rectangular prism   (d) triangular prism
   (e) triangular pyramid
3. (a) (i)   (b) (ii)   (c) (i)
4.

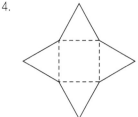

The Shape of Things

1 Use tracing paper to find two pairs of congruent shapes. Color each congruent pair a different color.

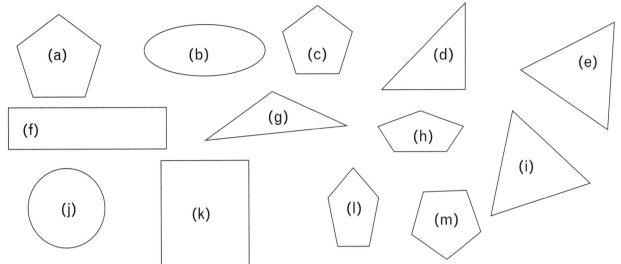

(a) (b) (c) (d) (e) (f) (g) (h) (i) (j) (k) (l) (m)

2 Match the shape to the correct name.

 (a) • • cube

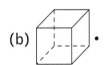 (b) • • square pyramid

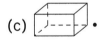 (c) • • triangular pyramid

 (d) • • triangular prism

 (e) • • rectangular prism

4 Draw the net for this shape.

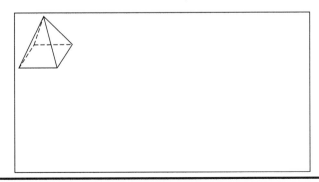

3 Circle the net that matches the model.

(a)

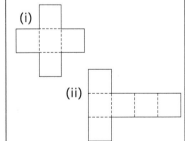
(i) (ii)

(b)

(i) (ii)

(c)
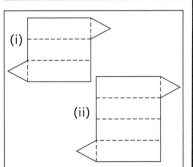
(i) (ii)

Chances

Learning Area Mathematics **Strand** Chance and Data	**Indicators** • Predicts, using laws of probability, the chances of certain colors being drawn. • Graphs and explains results.

Resources

• Each group to have an opaque bag of 12 identically shaped tokens (blocks, marbles, counters) of three colors in the ratio of 6:3:3; e.g., six red, three blue, three green

Lesson Plan and Organization

• Form groups of four or five students.

• Show students the contents of the bags, explaining the ratio of the three colors.

• Discuss the chances of each color being taken out; for example, red: 6 out of 24 (1 in 4), blue/green: 3 out of 24 (1 in 8).

• Students complete the "predictions" section of the worksheet, explaining the reason for their choice of number. On the graph, students color in their predictions.

• Explain the process for "data collection" and the rules.

  – Students take turns to remove a token from the bag. As they do so, the group scribe marks off the draw number. They also write a tally mark in the correct column each time a token of that color is removed.

  – Each student must return the token to the bag before it is passed to the next student.

• When all 24 draws are complete, the students color the results on the graph. How do they compare with the predictions?

• Explain to the students that the draw results will not necessarily be exactly in the ratio of 6:3:3, but there will always be a trend in that direction.

• Tally the totals for each color for the whole class. Over the larger sample, the 6:3:3 trend will be more evident.

• Ask students to complete the "How did it go?" section of the worksheet.

Additional Activities

• Students complete a whole-class graph of results and write explanations for the activity. Display the graph surrounded by the explanations.

• Students consider other options for repeating the activity and test them on each other.

Answers

Teacher check

Chances

Rules

- *You must have 12 tokens in the bag:*
  - *6 red tokens*
  - *3 blue tokens*
  - *3 green tokens*

- *Without looking, draw out one token and record the color.*
- *Put the token back in the bag for the next draw.*
- *Take turns.*

① Predictions

Out of the 24 draws, predict how many of each color will be drawn out and say why.

(a) Red [ ]

_____

(b) Blue [ ]

_____

(c) Green [ ]

_____

② Data collection (Cross off after each draw)

Draw tally		Red
1	13	
2	14	
3	15	total:
4	16	**Blue**
5	17	
6	18	
7	19	
8	20	total:
9	21	**Green**
10	22	
11	23	
12	24	total:

③ Graph (P = prediction, D = draw)

	P	D	P	D	P	D
24						
23						
22						
21						
20						
19						
18						
17						
16						
15						
14						
13						
12						
11						
10						
9						
8						
7						
6						
5						
4						
3						
2						
1						
	P	D	P	D	P	D
	Red		Blue		Green	

④ Evaluation

Was the result exactly as you predicted?   yes no

Saving Water

Learning Area

Science

Strands

Earth and Beyond

Indicators

- Understands the value of each person actively reducing his/her use of water for the benefit of all.
- Knows ways in which the use of water can be reduced.
- Knows devices which have been developed to help us reduce water use.

Resources

- Examples of water-saving devices, e.g., shower head, water timer (optional)
- Literature on the effects of water shortage (optional) note: these may be obtained by writing to the water authority in your city/state
- Literature and photographs of water-saving ideas and devices (optional)

Web Sites

- There are many sites available including:
  http://www.earthshare.org/tips/watersavingtips.html

Lesson Plan and Organization

- Give students the opportunity to browse through the resources and access the Internet for further information, if used.
- On the board, write ideas students have about the importance of using less water. Discuss their ideas. Students complete Question 1.
- On the board, write ideas for saving water that students have found from their research. Discuss the advantages and disadvantages of their suggestions. Students complete Question 2.
- Show the water-saving devices you have acquired (if being used) and explain how they work. Ask how many students employ these measures at home. Students complete Question 3.

Additional Activities

- Students choose a water-saving device to draw, label and describe to the class.
- Students design and color posters advocating the use of water-saving devices. These may be displayed throughout the school.
- Students collect data and graph the number of families using selected water-saving devices.
- Present all work in a display.

Answers

1. Teacher check
2. Teacher check
3. (a) water-saver shower head   (b) dual flush toilet
   (c) water timer   (d) Teacher check

Saving Water

1 Why is it important for us to use less water at home?

_____

_____

2 (a) Draw pictures to illustrate these great water-saving ideas.

Don't leave the rinse water running when washing the dishes. Fill one sink with rinse water.	Turn off the tap while brushing your teeth.

(b) Draw and write about two more of your own.

_____	_____

3 There are many different kinds of water-saving devices and fixtures. Label each device and explain how it saves water. Do one of your own.

dual flush toilet	water-saver shower head	water timer

(a)	Name: Description:	(b)	Name: Description:
(c)	Name: Description:	(d)	Name: Description:

Materials Close Up

Indicators

- Carefully observes physical characteristics of a material with and without a magnifying lens.
- Records observations by writing and drawing.
- Highlights the differences in what we see with and without an optical aid.

Resources

- Three lids or three pieces of colored card stock to place the materials on
- Small quantities of three common food samples; e.g., flour, coconut, salt, sugar, cocoa, coffee
- A hand magnifying lens for each student

Web Site

- History of microscopes:

  http://www.microscope-microscope.org/basic/microscope-history.htm

Lesson Plan and Organization

- Introduce and discuss each material to ensure students know what each is.
- Distribute the material, placing it on card stock or lid, ensuring the color of the card/lid is distinct from the color of the material.
- In groups, students orally describe their materials before drawing them and writing a description.
- Distribute the lenses and explain how to use them. It is better to view a small quantity of the material. Discuss how different the materials appear when magnified. Students complete Question 2.
- Discuss the differences the students have noted between viewing with the naked eye and with a magnifying lens. Students complete Question 3.

Additional Activities

- Repeat the study using different materials.
- Research the history of the magnifying glass.
- Study simple recipes using the materials. Bake and share!
- Use the lens to count the grains in a square inch of material.
- Write an imaginative story based on a microscopic character; for example, "My Life As a Microbe" or "I Was Shrunk."
- Present all work in a display.

Answers

Teacher check

Materials Close Up

Without the Lens

1 Draw and describe each material.

(a) _____

_____

_____

(b) _____

_____

_____

(c) _____

_____

_____

With the Lens

2 Draw and describe each material.

(a) _____

_____

_____

(b) _____

_____

_____

(c) _____

_____

_____

3 (a) Which material changed the most
when you looked at it through the lens? _____

(b) What was so different about it? _____

4 Write two things about the materials that looked different under the lens.

_____

Medicines

<table>
<tr><td>

Learning Area

Health

Strands

Concepts for a Healthy
Lifestyle

</td></tr>
</table>

Indicators

- Understands that different medicines come in a range of packaging.
- Appreciates the safety packaging features of some medicine containers.
- Realizes the dangers of misusing medicines.

Resources

- Collection of medicine packages
- Library resources on medicines; how to store and dispose of them, etc.
- Internet access

Lesson Plan and Organization

- Introduce the medicine packages, one at a time. Discuss what they are, when they might be used, who might use them. Look at the instructions for use; how many times a day the medicine is to be taken or applied, quantities, maximum dose, etc. Highlight distinguishing features of medicine packages, notably safety lids and warnings. Discuss what such features mean and why they are necessary.
- Discuss medicines students are familiar with, either for themselves or family members.
- Read through and answer cloze procedure with students. Discuss any unfamiliar vocabulary.
- Students complete the worksheet.

Additional Activities

- Students write or role-play stories involving the use of medicines.
- Students relate personal experiences with medicines.
- Students design and make a medicine package.
- On their next visit, students record types of medicines and packages available at a local supermarket.

Answers

1. 1. medicines   2. illness   3. prevent   4. many   5. tablets   6. different   7. bottles   8. counter   9. supermarkets   10. prescription

2.– 4. Teacher check

5. (a) capsules   (b) chest rub   (c) cough syrup   (d) drops   (e) inhaler   (f) ointment

Medicines

1 Use the correct word in the spaces. Use each word once only.

<table>
<tr><td>

Word Bank

counter

prescription

illness

prevent

many

different

tablets

bottles

supermarkets

medicines

</td></tr>
</table>

People use m_____[1] to help them recover from an i_____[2] or disease. Medicine can also be taken to p_____[3] an illness or disease.

There are m_____[4] different types of medicine. They can be liquids, t_____[5], ointments or gases. They come in many d_____[6] types of packages, such as b_____[7], tubes, boxes and inhalers.

Some medicines can be bought over the c_____[8] at pharmacies or s_____[9], but some can only be bought with a p_____[10] from a doctor.

2 List two ways you could recognize a medicine container.

(a) _____ (b) _____

3 Write one common warning you will find on a medicine package.

_____

4 Explain what this warning means and why it is written on the package.

_____

_____

5 Match these labels to the medicines below.

| capsules | ointment | chest rub | cough syrup | drops | inhaler |

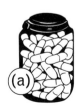 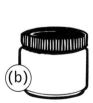  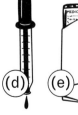 

(a)   (b)   (c)   (d)   (e)   (f)

Sun-Safe Poster Plan

Learning Area

Health

Strands

Concepts for a Healthy Lifestyle

Indicators

- Understands the need for "sun-safe" awareness.
- Uses ideas for sun safety to produce an informative poster.
- Knows the dangers of overexposure to the sun.

Resources

- Library or community resources on sun safety (optional)
- Poster-making materials, e.g., magazines, paper, posterboard, pens
- Internet access (optional)

Web Sites

- Type "The Sun and Sun Safety" into the search engine for a list of sites.

Lesson Plan and Organization

- Brainstorm to ascertain the knowledge and ideas students already have on the sun and sun safety. Record this information on the board.
- Introduce the task and brainstorm to list ideas for a poster. Look at the worksheet together and consider the suggested ideas. Any resources collected may be viewed (if used). Students start their designs.
- Approve plans, giving ideas for improvements if necessary, before allowing students to start work on their posters.

Additional Activities

- Students research a project on the sun and/or the solar system.
- Compile a list of "sun" vocabulary to be used in poetry writing.
- Create a "sun-safe" board game.
- Create models of the sun or artwork about the sun.
- Write poems about being sun-safe or about the sun.

Answers

Teacher check

Sun-Safe Poster Plan

Design Brief

Plan and complete a poster about sun-safe ideas.

Materials

- Large sheet of art paper
- Magazines to cut out
- Internet pictures
- Pens

Steps

1. Draw a plan showing your layout.
2. Check off the items on the checklist as you include them.
3. Collect pictures from magazines or the Internet.
4. Complete your poster on art paper, following your plan.

Checklist

Title of the poster ◯

Drawings of your own ◯

Cut-out pictures ◯

Labels for the pictures ◯

Border ◯

Ideas to Include on Your Poster

The Sun
- The sun gives off dangerous ultraviolet rays.
- It causes cancers, wrinkling, freckles and burns.
- It is so bright it can damage your eyes.

Sunscreen
- SPF means "Sun Protection Factor."
- SPF should be 30+.
- Apply sunscreen about 20 minutes before going out in the sun.

Sunglasses
- Polarized lenses help protect the eyes from the harmful sun's rays.

Hats
- Wear a wide-brimmed hat.
- Always wear a hat when going out in the sun.

Clothing
- Cover up as much as possible when going into the sun.
- Wear long sleeves and stay in the shade.

Famous Tower/Bridge Project

Learning Area

Society and Environment

Strands

Place and Space

Indicators

- Works to an agreed project format.
- Researches information from a variety of sources.
- Records information in a range of formats.

Resources

- School/local library resources
- Tower/bridge posters, pamphlets, magazines and photographs
- Project presentation material (card stock for cover, colored backing paper for each page)
- Internet access
- Blank world map for each student

Web Sites

- Try these sites:

  Tower Bridge
  http://www.towerbridge.org.uk

  Tower of London
  http://www.tower-of-london.com/

  Leaning Tower of Pisa
  http://torre.duomo.pisa.it/

  Sydney Harbour Bridge
  http://www.harbourbridge.com.au

  Brooklyn Bridge
  http://www.endex.com/gf/buildings/bbridge/bbridge.html

  Golden Gate Bridge
  http://www.goldengatebridge.org/

  Eiffel Tower
  http://www.tour-eiffel.fr/teiffel/uk/

Lesson Plan and Organization

- Brainstorm to list the names of world famous landmarks.

- Look at the examples of bridges and towers at the top of the worksheet. Ascertain what the students already know about them; their construction, their history, why they are famous. Has anyone visited them, seen them on TV or in movies?
- Each student will be completing a project on a chosen structure. Work through the project headings listed on the worksheet, ensuring all students understand what is required.
- Students choose a tower or bridge to research. To ease pressure on book resources, ensure four or five students are researching each of the seven structures. This will also provide a more balanced project display.
- Tell students to note the sources of all their information for the bibliography at the end of the project. It will also make it easier for them to locate the information later, if necessary.
- Students begin their research, using all the resources available to them. Allow them to work in groups, encouraging discussion and sharing of information.

Additional Activities

- Students give oral presentations about their chosen landmark, using their completed projects, to the class and other classes.
- Students research more about the city in which their chosen structure stands.
- Students make a model or a collage of a structure.
- Students paint or draw a poster advertising the structure.
- Present all work in a display.
- Students research another world famous landmark.

Answers

Teacher check

Famous Tower/Bridge Project

1 Select one of these famous towers or bridges to research.

- **Tower of London** (England)
- **Tower Bridge** (England)
- **Eiffel Tower** (France)
- **Leaning Tower of Pisa** (Italy)

- **Brooklyn Bridge** (USA)
- **Golden Gate Bridge** (USA)
- **Sydney Harbour Bridge** (Australia)

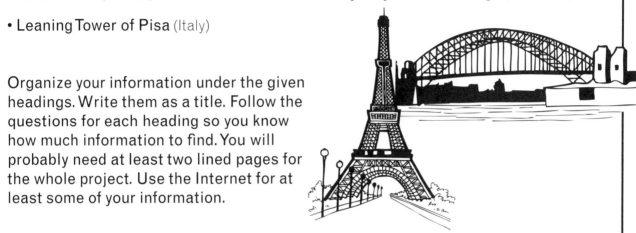

2 Organize your information under the given headings. Write them as a title. Follow the questions for each heading so you know how much information to find. You will probably need at least two lined pages for the whole project. Use the Internet for at least some of your information.

- -

Famous Tower/Bridge Project Plan

3 Present your work as a project, following the guidelines below. Check each section as you complete it.

Cover .... ○
    include the structure's name, photo/ drawing, your name, date and class.

Headings .... ○

Structure .... ○
    Do your own drawing of the structure. Label it.

Location .... ○
    Where is it found? Label the country and city on the world map.

Size .... ○
    What are the dimensions of your structure? List some.

Material .... ○
    What is it made of? List the materials, explaining which are the main ones.

Age .... ○
    When was it built? Tell how old it is. How long did it take to build?

Use .... ○
    What are the main uses of the structure? Write at least two sentences.

Other interesting facts .... ○
    What other interesting facts did you find out about the structure?
        – How much did it cost to build?
        – What interesting things have happened to it over the years?
        – Have any famous people had anything to do with it?

Visiting .... ○
    Have you visited this structure? Do you know anyone who has?
    Ask them what they thought about it. Include any photos you or they may have taken.

Bibliography .... ○
    List all the resources you have used: title and author of books; Internet URLs, etc.

Production Systems

<table>
<tr><td>

Learning Area

Society and Environment

Strands

Resources

</td><td>

Indicators

- Researches information from a variety of sources.
- Selects relevant information for project.
- Uses a simple production chain template to record information.

</td></tr>
</table>

Resources

- School/local library resources of possible product choices (these may be collected after students have made their product choices.)
- Posters, pamphlets, magazines and photographs relating to products
- Internet access

Lesson Plan and Organization

- This lesson will require research, by the teacher, on the production systems of some common products familiar to the students; e.g., flour, paper, yarn, dairy products.
  Break the production process into five main stages:

  Stage 1   Collection and storage of raw materials.

  Stages 2 – 4   Processing. (This will vary for each product. Keep simple. Include major points only.)

  Stage 5   Packaging and delivery.

  The main thing for the students to appreciate is that raw materials are treated in various ways before the product, as we know it, is produced. The five stages of the production chain should be displayed on the board.

- Discuss with students possible examples for their research. Limit their choices to **basic products** and approve them before they begin their research. These may include: plastic, frozen vegetables, coffee, steel, paper, wooden furniture, soft drinks, etc.

- Depending on resources available, it may be simpler to have a list of processes from which the students choose.

- Students write research information on a spare sheet of paper or the back of the worksheet.

Additional Activities

- Present completed projects to the class and other classes, as an oral presentation, with a labeled model, informative talk or a book. Oral presentations may be videotaped or photographed.

- Students research further specific aspects of their process; e.g., wool – different breeds of sheep/goats/llamas producing different types of wool.

- Compile a list of topic spelling words relating to a list of projects, occupations and associated words.

Answers

Teacher check

Production Systems

Systems are used to produce goods that people need; for example, a wool sweater.

1 Use a simple production chain to show how your product is produced. Plan the five stages of its production carefully. Draw and label each stage.

Product name:

(a) _____

(b) _____

(c) _____

_____

(e) _____

(d) _____

2 List the jobs of four people who help make your product.

(a) _____

(b) _____

(c) _____

(d) _____

3 Draw and label two different ways your product can be used.

(a) _____

(b) _____

Explorer Research

Learning Area
Society and Environment
Strands
Time, Continuity and Change
Investigation, Communication and Participation

Indicators

• Researches information from a variety of sources.

• Selects relevant information for a project.

• Records information as a report.

Resources

• Background information about each explorer would be beneficial

• Bulk school/local library loan of resources relating to these explorers

• Class world map and globe

• Internet access

Web Sites

• Search for "voyages of exploration" or individual explorers.

Lesson Plan and Organization

• Discuss the explorers to ascertain how much the students know about each. Identify the places visited and the routes taken by each on a large world map or globe. Use this map as the backdrop for a display of student work.

• Divide the class into six groups and give each an explorer to research.

• Students work together, collating information from available resources which they will discuss before completing their worksheets.

• The illustration for Question 7 may be done in pencil.

Additional Activities

• Students in each group choose one of their illustrations (in Question 7) to enlarge and work on together to produce, using a range of materials.

• Students write and perform a short play depicting an interesting and exciting event from one of the explorer's voyages.

• Students plan how to present their work orally, with each group member participating.

• Students write stories of the voyages, casting themselves as the explorer.

• Students produce a time line to include all explorers and their voyages. Each group is responsible for adding information about its explorer.

• Present all work in a display.

Answers

Teacher check

Explorer Research

1 Select an explorer from the list below and complete the information.

Name of Explorer

• Marco Polo

• Christopher Columbus

• Vasco Da Gama

• Sir Francis Drake

• James Cook

• Ferdinand Magellan

2 About your explorer

(a) Birth date: _____

(b) Country of birth: _____

(c) Childhood information: _____

_____

_____

3 Draw and label two things he brought back from his explorations.

(a) _____   (b) _____

4 His exploration:

(a) Where did he go? Explain one of his journeys.

_____

_____

_____

_____

(b) List some things he learned.

_____

_____

_____

5 Draw and label an illustration that would be appropriate for a book about your explorer.

Name Label

Learning Area

Technology

Strands

Technology Process

Indicators

- Designs a label conforming to the brief.
- Follows design to make full-size label.
- Evaluates final product and process.

Resources

- Card stock and a selection of writing materials
- Computer typeface list (optional)
- Scraps of material and yarn, etc.

Lesson Plan and Organization

- Discuss the design brief and explain where the labels will be used (on drawers, bulletin board, window). This will help students determine the size of label required.
- Students draw a classroom plan and highlight the intended position of the labels.
- Discuss the range of typefaces available (freehand, stencils and computer) and the associated advantages and disadvantages of each.
- Students design their labels and describe how they will use the materials.
- Students work out the size of label required and relate it to the scale of their plan.
- Students make their labels, display them in the agreed position and complete the evaluation section on the worksheet.

Additional Activities

- Display labels as required; e.g., on the months of the year, class birthdays, to identify monitors.
- Students create other labels for books, posters, etc.
- Categorize labels in a variety of ways; for example, materials used, heights, typefaces used.

Answers

Teacher check

Name Label

Design Brief

Plan and produce a name label that can be clearly seen from across the room.

1 Draw a plan of where your name label will be located in the room.

2 Draw a plan of your name label design. Show all the design features you are going to use on your label.

You will need to:

- Measure the size needed.
- Write your name using a special typeface.
- Make the label and decorate it.
- Attach your name label where it is to go.

Use:

- A sheet of paper or card stock.
- Colored pencils, crayons, or markers.
- Special designs to add to your label.

Label Design

Evaluation

1 Write the measurements of your label: _____ wide x _____ high

2 (a) Can you read your name on your label from:

(i) right in front of it? ◯ yes ◯ no

(ii) Three yards away? ◯ yes ◯ no

(b) Do you consider your label a success? ◯ yes ◯ no

Why? _____

_____

3 How many colors did you use to decorate the label? _____

4 On the back of this sheet, write about any problems you had with this label or any changes needed.

The Kitchen Hand Tool

Learning Area
Technology

Strands
Technology Process

Materials

Indicators
- Carefully studies the designs and materials of some kitchen appliances.
- Studies, in detail, the mechanisms of these devices.
- Considers the energy source for the appliances.

Resources
- A kitchen implement (electric or manual) brought in by each student; e.g., beater, spatula, can opener, egg slicer, garlic press, whisk, wooden spoon

Web Sites
- Students could research the origins of their particular device; e.g., wooden spoons.

  http://www.reluctantgourmet.com/wooden_spoons.htm

Lesson Plan and Organization
- In groups, students describe their implements, including the materials they are made from, how they are used and for what tasks. They identify the source of energy required to make them work; e.g., electricity, manual.

- Students look carefully at their kitchen appliances and consider why they have been designed in that way, using those particular materials. For example, consider the size of the handles – they must accommodate the size of an adult hand; the material from which a spatula is made, plastic – the head must be soft enough to allow it to bend, the handle strong enough to take the strain of manipulating the head, and so on.

- How old is the implement? This may have implications for the materials used. Do they last? Do they break or wear out easily? Do metal components rust or tarnish with constant washing? Could an alternative material be used?

- Students complete the worksheet, taking particular care in Question 3 to draw an accurate representation of the device.

- In Question 6, students consider how well their devices perform. Encourage them to consider possible improvements in material or design.

Additional Activities
- Students present talks on their appliances, using worksheets as a plan.

- Students research the history of their appliance, cost of appliance, etc.

- Display appliances and worksheets.

- Students write a story, "A Day in the Life of a ...," using their appliances as the subject of the story.

- Students make a list of small kitchen appliances commonly in use today. Ask parents, grandparents and great-grandparents which implements were available in their youth. From this information, students create a time chart to show how things have changed.

Answers
Teacher check

The Kitchen Hand Tool

Your tool:

1 List two jobs this tool does.

(a) _____ (b) _____

2 Check the energy source which makes the tool work.

○ electricity ○ manual ○ (other) _____

3 Carefully draw and label a picture of your tool. Include a label for the materials it is made from.

4 Explain how it works.

_____

_____

_____

_____

_____

_____

_____

_____

_____

_____

5 List three parts of the tool, the materials they are made from, and why each material was used.

Part	Material	Why was this material chosen?
(a)		
(b)		
(c)		

6 (a) Rate how well your tool works.

hopeless ○—○—○—○—○—○—○—○ great

(b) What improvements (if any) could be made?

_____

_____

Package It

Learning Area
Technology

Strands
Technology Process

Indicators

• Learns how a box is put together using overlaps.

• Learns the information which must be included on the packaging.

• Designs the cover of a box for a specific product.

Resources

• A small, empty, cardboard box for each student to open out; e.g., cardboard medicine boxes, small food containers, milk cartons

• Thin card stock or construction paper to trace the net of the box

• Colored pencils, fine-point pens, scissors, adhesive tape, glue, etc.

• List of computer typefaces (optional)

Lesson Plan and Organization

• In groups, students invent products which will be packaged in the boxes they are going to make. They discuss types of products that would be suitable. Students should also consider the suitability of the size of the box. For example, flour is generally used in fairly large quantities, so a container the size of a gelatin box would be far too small, even though the material would be suitable.

• Students carefully open up their boxes and lay them flat to reveal their nets and overlaps, taking care to pry the boxes apart on the overlap side to retain an undamaged net.

• Discuss the nets of the boxes, which are all rectangular prisms: How many faces, the shape and size of each face, similar/congruent faces? Students draw a small scale of the box net on the worksheet and number the sides.

• Students discuss what they will put on each side of the box (name of product, additional

information, etc.) and complete Question 3 in the design brief. Students may draw draft sketches of their designs before putting them on the worksheet.

• Students carefully draw around their nets on card stock or construction paper.

• Ensuring the orientation is correct, students draw their designs onto the faces of their nets and color them.

• Students cut out the nets and carefully score the lines to give sharp creases. Finally, they construct the boxes by folding and gluing the overlaps.

• In groups, students discuss how successful their box-making has been before completing the evaluation section at the bottom of the page.

Additional Activities

• Research box-making as a topic using the Internet and books for reference.

• Group the "products" into categories and construct a mini-store.

• Calculate the total volume of the boxes.

• Students write an advertisement for their product. This could be audio- or videotaped.

Answers

Teacher check

Package It

Design Brief

Make and label a box for your own product.

1 Open a box and draw the shape of the net.

2 Number the six sides of the net.

┌─ **Net** ─────────────────────────┐
│   │
│   │
│   │
│   │
│   │
└────────────────────────────────────┘

3 Plan what you want to put on each side. Use a special typeface for your labels if you wish.

Include:

◯ barcode.

◯ product name and logo.

◯ manufacturer's address.

◯ ingredients.

◯ descriptions.

Side design plan

side 1	side 2	side 3
side 4	**side 5**	**side 6**

4 Trace your box onto the card stock.

5 Draw what you planned for each side and color it in.

6 Cut out and make your box.

Evaluation

1 Rate your box. How well did it go?

◯───◯───◯───◯───◯───◯───◯───◯

hopeless   great

2 Why did you choose that rating? _____

_____

Clay Monster

Learning Area
Arts and Technology

Strands
Communicating Art Ideas
Technology Process

Indicators
- Designs a character, considering material to be used.
- Makes character from design.
- Evaluates finished product.

Resources
- Modeling clay or similar material
- Modeling tools; e.g., fine and broad sticks, rags, water
- Newspaper
- Paints
- Literature about monsters (optional)

Web Site
- Research monsters in literature:
  http://www.wsu.edu/~delahoyd/monsters.html

Lesson Plan and Organization
- Present the topic by reading literature which includes a monster as a main character. Encourage students to tell stories they know.
- List the names of monsters from fiction.
- Discuss the set task and introduce the medium and materials they will be using.
- In groups, students discuss plans for monsters, decide upon their individual choice, then make their clay monster.
- In groups, students discuss how they feel about their own and each other's monsters before completing the evaluation section of the worksheet.

Additional Activities
- Students write "Monster" poems or stories to describe their monsters.
- Students develop a class "Monster Mass" graph, recording the mass of each monster.
- Students research monsters in literature and compile a book list for the class.
- Display the monsters.
- Present monster "show and tell" to other classes.

Answers
Teacher check

Clay Monster

Design Brief

Design and create a 3-D monster using clay.

1 Check each section as you include it:

○ body shape

○ legs/feet/paws to stand on

○ face

○ eyes

○ ears

○ nose

○ mouth

○ skin covering/hair/feathers

○ wings/antennae/claws

○ pose (standing up/lying down/ sitting/other)

Evaluation

1 Answer yes or no, then explain your answer.

(a) Does your finished monster look different from your design?   ○ yes   ○ no

(b) Did you have any problems making your monster?   ○ yes   ○ no

(c) Did you make any changes to your original design?   ○ yes   ○ no

2 (a) Rate your finished monster.

○——○——○——○——○——○——○——○
hopeless   great

(b) Give reasons for your rating.

Color Wheel

Learning Area

The Arts

Strands

Using Art Skills, Techniques and Processes

Indicators

- Learns the primary colors and how they combine to make other colors.
- Uses imagination and knowledge of colors in the natural world to name manufactured colors.

Resources

- Newspaper, brushes, water
- Palette or art paper for mixing colors
- Red, blue and yellow paints
- Copy of color wheel

Lesson Plan and Organization

- Prepare the color wheels. Either provide each student with the worksheet as it is or, enlarge the worksheet to tabloid size paper.

- Students carefully paint the red, blue and yellow segments of the wheel, cleaning the brush between colors.

- Using their palettes or art paper, students mix two adjacent primary colors in graduated amounts for the three segments between the two colors. For example, mixing red and blue:

  Segment 2 = more red than blue.

  Segment 3 = equal amounts of red and blue.

  Segment 4 = more blue than red.

- Students paint the segments, taking care that the paint on one segment is dry before painting an adjacent segment. When finished, the wheel should show a graduated change of color. Allow to dry completely.

- Students answer the questions at the bottom of the page. In Question 2, students can create their own names; e.g., autumn yellow, sunset red.

- Ask students to find things in the classroom which match the colors they have made.

Additional Activities

- Students research famous works of art to try to match their colors.

- Students use prisms to study rainbows.

- Students write a report of the activity and include photographs and captions about the activity.

- Display the reports, photographs and color wheels.

Answers

1. Teacher check

2. 1, 5, 9

3–4. Teacher check

Color Wheel

❶ Mix the colors as directed and complete the color wheel.

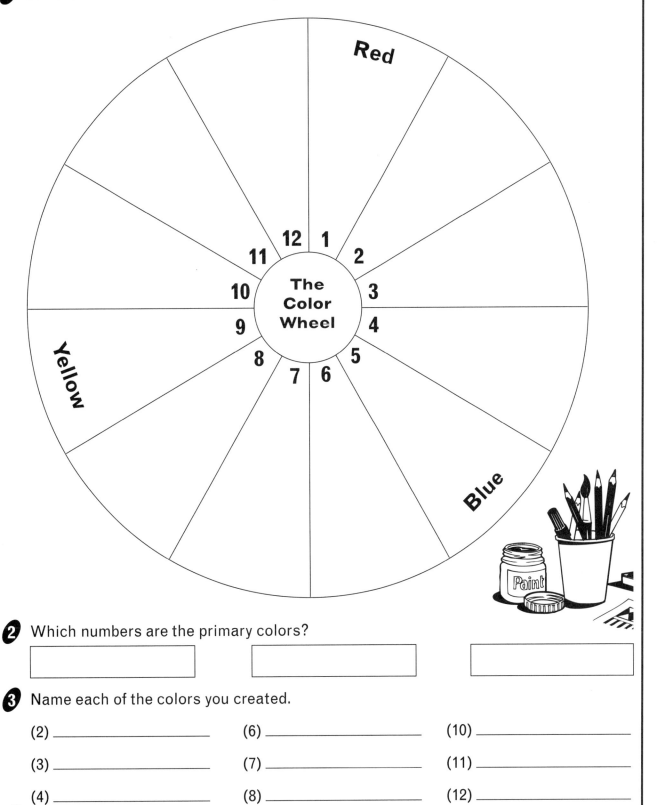

❷ Which numbers are the primary colors?

❸ Name each of the colors you created.

(2) _____   (6) _____   (10) _____

(3) _____   (7) _____   (11) _____

(4) _____   (8) _____   (12) _____

❹ Match your colors with an object in the room; write the objects and colors on the back of this sheet.

Insect Words

Learning Area
English

Strands
Reading and Writing

Indicators

- Learns the different body parts of an insect.
- Learns characteristics of different insects.
- Spells insect topic words correctly.

Resources

- Library resources on insects (optional)
- Internet access for research (optional)

Lesson Plan and Organization

- Introduce the subject by ascertaining what students already know about insects.
- Begin a topic word list by writing keywords on the board. Define and discuss words.
- Show students pictures/posters of insects. Briefly describe and ask questions about them.
- Look at the list of topic words on the worksheet. Check off any already mentioned, define and discuss the rest. Ask students to add three topic words of their own.
- Read through the rest of the worksheet to ensure instructions are clear. In Question 1, explain the spelling rules for changing verb tense where appropriate.
- Students complete the worksheet.
- Test the students on the insect words, partner-test the last three words added by the student.

Additional Activities

- Students read their sentences aloud.
- Students make models or draw pictures of insects with all body parts labeled and their functions described.
- Students compile a list of insects and how they move. The results may be categorized.
- Students can mime insects and their movements for others to guess.

Answers

1. (a) crawling, crawled, crawls
    (b) creeping, crept, creeps
    (c) hopping, hopped, hops
    (d) scuttling, scuttled, scuttles
    (e) gliding, glided, glides
(Creep doesn't follow the rule.)

2.

A	B	D	O	M	E	N	X	abdomen
C	M	A	F	D	M	X	U	cicada
C	I	C	A	D	A	P	R	thorax
A	N	T	E	N	N	A	H	antenna
M	G	B	E	E	T	L	E	wasp
D	S	C	C	Z	I	W	A	beetle
N	P	N	W	A	S	P	D	head
T	H	O	R	A	X	O	H	mantis
								wings

3.

body parts	moving words	Insect names
abdomen	creeping	cicada
thorax	flying	wasp
antenna	running	beetle
head	hopping	mantis
wings	crawling	grasshopper
		butterfly

4. Teacher check

Insect Words

Topic Words

insect

thorax

creeping

grasshopper

butterfly

head

flying

running

abdomen

mantis

cicada

hopping

crawling

wasp

antenna

beetle

wings

_____

_____

_____

1 Add endings to these words that describe how an insect moves. Circle the word that doesn't follow the rule.

	-ing	**-ed**	**-s**
(a) crawl			
(b) creep			
(c) hop			
(d) scuttle			
(e) glide			

2 Find the nine list words. Write them as you find them.

A	B	D	O	M	E	N	X
C	W	A	F	D	M	X	U
C	I	C	A	D	A	P	R
A	N	T	E	N	N	A	H
M	G	B	E	E	T	L	E
D	S	C	C	Z	I	W	A
N	P	N	W	A	S	P	D
T	H	O	R	A	X	O	H

_____

_____

_____

_____

_____

_____

_____

_____

_____

3 Write all the insect words in the correct group. Remember to include your three words.

body parts	moving words	insect names

4 Use each pair of words in a sentence.

(a) cicada, crawling _____

(b) abdomen, butterfly _____

Insect Problems

<table>
<tr><td>

Learning Area

Mathematics

Strands

Number
Space

</td><td>

Indicator

• Uses knowledge of insect anatomy to calculate math problems.

</td></tr>
</table>

Resources

• Library resources on insects (optional)

• Calculator for each student

Lesson Plan and Organization

• Introduce the subject by ascertaining what students already know about insects.

• Discuss similarities and differences of anatomy between insects.

• Work through examples similar to Questions 1 and 2 on the worksheet.

• Students complete Question 3 using sharp lead and colored pencils.

Additional Activities

• Students draw and write cartoon problems similar to those in Question 2 (b). These may be shared for other students to complete.

• Using library resources for factual information, students may write some of their own insect problems.

• Insect pictures from Question 3 may be enlarged, colored and displayed together with library resources.

Answers

1. (a) 3,852   (b) 110   (c) 2,000   (d) 7,700   (e) 86   (f) 1,000   (g) 7,434

   (h) 180   (i) 25 weeks/6.25 months   (j) 168

2. (a) Teacher check   (b) 36

3. Teacher check

Insect Problems

1 Insect calculations

(a) How many legs are there on 642 butterflies?

_____ legs

(b) If I found 220 beetle antennae, how many beetles would they be from?

_____ beetles

(c) 10,000 bees live in 5 hives; how many in each hive?

_____ bees

(d) If a moth laid 1,100 eggs each day, how many would she lay in a week?

_____ eggs

(e) I saw 17 ants on a rosebush, 26 on the path and 43 on the rocks; how many ants did I see altogether?

_____ ants

(f) On Monday, 345 bees hatched, on Tuesday, only 187 hatched and on Wednesday, 468 hatched in the bee nursery. How many bees hatched altogether?

_____ bees

(g) An ant nest had 9,782 ants, but it flooded with water so 2,348 moved away. How many were left in the nest?

_____ ants

(h) A beetle has 4 wings. How many wings will 45 beetles have?

_____ wings

(i) If a spider ate 4 flies a week, how long would it take to eat 100 flies?

_____ weeks

(j) I found 56 ants stuck on my toast yesterday; today I found twice as many. How many have I found altogether?

_____ ants

2 Ant fractions

(a) Give $^3/_4$ of these ants leaves to carry.

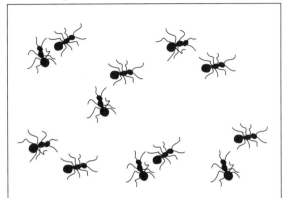

(b)

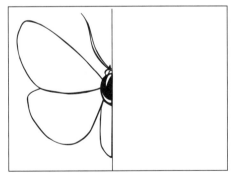

Oh no! Half my ants are dead. I only have 18 now!

How many ants did he have to start with?

_____ ants

3 Draw the other half of these insects to show their symmetry.

(a)

(b)

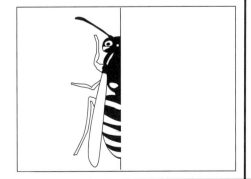

Insect Camouflage

Learning Area

English

Strands

Reading

Indicators

- Understands the term "camouflage."
- Learns how insects use camouflage to hide from predators and prey.

Resources

- Library resources on insects (optional)
- Internet access for research (optional)

Web Site

- http://science.howstuffworks.com/animal-camouflage1.htm

Lesson Plan and Organization

- Introduce the subject by ascertaining what students already know about insect camouflage. Discuss how it helps animals survive.

- Draw up a table of the insects mentioned in the text, what camouflage they use, and how it helps them as predator or prospective prey.

- Read the information text at the top of the page or ask selected students to read it aloud. Discuss the content and compare to the information on the board.

- Students complete Questions 1 to 6 on the worksheet. Question 7 may be completed on the back of the worksheet.

Additional Activities

- Students research the topic further using the Internet and library resources.

- Students draw or paint an insect using camouflage.

- Display artwork and resources.

Answers

1. to blind or veil

2. It uses camouflage to look like a dry twig, sits very still then grabs its prey as it wanders close by.

3. to look like real leaves

4. (a) camouflage   (b) conceal   (c) veil

5. Teacher check

6. (a) to protect themselves   (b) to catch their prey

7. Teacher check

Insect Camouflage

Camouflage is used by insects to conceal themselves from their enemies or their prey. The word "camouflage" is French and means "to blind or veil."

In order to protect themselves, some insects use color and shape. Sometimes, they use color to hide so their predators can't see them. Grasshoppers use their color to hide in the grass and butterflies often blend in to the colors of their resting places.

Sometimes, they just look like something else. Leaf insects are leaf-shaped and actually sway gently to look just like leaves. Some insects may display warning colors to predators. Some moths have colorful designs on their wings that look like the eyes of a large animal. Some caterpillars can scare birds by showing bright colors. Insects may also resemble another insect which is not very nice to eat, or they may make themselves look like bird droppings, as some moths do. For these insects it is much better to be missed by a predator than to have to fight to stay alive.

Camouflage is also used by insects to catch their prey. A praying mantis may be the same color and shape as a dry twig. It will sit very still until an insect wanders close by, then it grabs it.

Because insects are eaten by such a large number of animals, disguise is important to them.

1 What does camouflage mean? _____

2 How does a praying mantis catch its food? _____

_____

3 Why do leaf insects sway gently? _____

_____

4 List three words from the story which mean "to hide."

5 Describe two ways that insects use camouflage.

(a) _____

(b) _____

6 Give two reasons why insects use camouflage.

(a) _____

_____

(b) _____

_____

7 On a separate sheet, draw a praying mantis using camouflage to catch its prey.

My Life as an Insect

Learning Area English	**Indicators** • Uses previous knowledge of insects and library resources to write an imaginative story. • Plans a story before writing.
Strands Writing	

Resources
• Library resources on insects (optional)

Lesson Plan and Organization
• Students may use the worksheet to write the final copy of a poem, short story or acrostic using a familiar insect word.

• Discuss various plans to refresh the students' memories. Include content to be used; "Who am I?," "Where do I live?," "What happens?," ending, etc.

• Students write a first draft on a separate sheet of paper or the back of their worksheet.

• In pairs, students read each other's plan and offer positive criticism for improvement.

• Students write final copy of story onto the illustrated worksheet.

Additional Activities
• Students choose an insect to draw in detail to accompany their story, or an illustration about their writing.

• Students write an insect poem.

• Students write a short project on their chosen insect.

• Display all work and resources.

Answers
Teacher check

Insect Observation

Learning Area

Science

Strands

Life and Living

Indicators

- Recognizes different insects.
- Observes anatomy and movement of chosen insect.
- Compares data collected.

Resources

- Library resources on insects (optional)
- Appropriate insect container
- Magnifying glasses
- A small insect collected carefully from the garden

Web Sites

- http://insected.arizona.edu/info.htm
- http://www.earthlife.net/insects/six.html
- http://www.ivyhall.district96.k12.il.us/4th/kkhp/1insects/bugmenu.html

Lesson Plan and Organization

- Discuss the characteristics of insects.
- Read through the worksheet.
- Discuss rules for collecting insects and treating them gently. Reinforce the need to stay away from spiders.
- Collect insects. (All insects should be treated carefully and released at the end of the lesson.)
- Students complete the worksheet, accurately recording what they observe.
- Question 2 should be completed using pencil and colored later. Labels should be included.
- Release insects as soon as possible.
- Choose selected students to share their work with the class.

Additional Activities

- Students use the planning sheet as a basis for a project on insects.
- Students complete Internet research on their particular insect.
- Students play "What am I?," describing features of a particular insect.
- Students create 3-D insect art using available materials, or complete large sketches of other insects.
- Display all work with library resources as part of a unit about insects.

Answers

Teacher check

Insect Observation

Insect Name

1 How many of each does your insect have?

    (a) legs _____   (b) wings _____   (c) body parts _____   (d) antennae _____

2 Use the magnifying glass to accurately draw the details of your creature.

3 Describe how your insect moves.

_____

_____

_____

4 Which of these describes the texture and shape of its body? (You can check more than one.)

texture: ◯ hairy   ◯ smooth   ◯ shiny   ◯ wrinkly   ◯ rough

               ◯ other _____

shape: ◯ long   ◯ short   ◯ wide   ◯ thin   ◯ fat

               ◯ tall   ◯ other _____

5 Special features (e.g., body parts, habits, protection):

_____

_____

_____

Insect Model

Learning Area

Technology

Strands

Technology process

Indicators

- Uses knowledge of insect anatomy to design and make an imaginary insect using scrap materials.

- Uses imagination and knowledge of scientific naming procedures to name model.

Resources

- Library resources on insects (optional)
- Collection of scrap material for model-making; e.g., egg cartons, colored candy wrappers, corks
- Supply of construction resources; e.g., pipe cleaners, string, glue, paints
- Newspaper

Web Sites

- Information on scientific names:
  http://www.xs4all.nl/~sbpoley/scinames.htm

- Information on insect parts:
  http://www.bijlmakers.com/entomology/bodypart.htm
  http://www.kidfish.bc.ca/ianatomy.htm

Lesson Plan and Organization

- Discuss the use of Latin for scientific names and classification; e.g., *Orientalis blatta* (oriental cockroach), *Bombus sp*. (bumble bee). Give examples of imaginary names that sound authentically scientific yet simply describe the physical appearance of an object; e.g., *Albus maximus* (large white insect), *Rubus scuttlus* (red, scuttling insect).
- Students plan their models using the materials available to them.
- Students construct their models and give them a scientific name.
- Students complete the assessment on the worksheet.

Additional Activities

- Students write a full description of their model insects, including habitat, life cycle, predators and prey/ food. These may be presented as short talks to the class.
- Students write a procedure explaining how their models were made. These may be presented orally to the class and should include solutions to the construction problems, etc.
- Display work in the class with the resources and worksheets. Models may be hung if they have wings!

Answers

Teacher check

Insect Model

Design Brief

Using your knowledge of insect features, design and build your own imaginary insect using scrap materials.

1 Draw your insect and label all the parts with the material to be used.

2 Check each part as you include it in your plan.

◯ two antennae

◯ a head

◯ a thorax

◯ an abdomen

◯ some wings

◯ six legs

◯ two eyes

3 Scientific name of your insect:

4 Make your insect as you planned.

- -

Evaluation

1 Rate how successful your model was.

◯—◯—◯—◯—◯—◯—◯—◯

hopeless   great

2 Did you have to make any changes as you were making it?   ◯ yes   ◯ no

Why? _____

3 Describe what you did that is different from your plan.

_____

4 Tell about any changes or ideas you'd like to try.

_____

_____

A HEALTHY LIFESTYLE

What Can I Do to Improve My Lifestyle?

Very few of us have a perfectly healthy lifestyle. There's room for improvement for all of us. Some things are easy to change, while others are more difficult.

1. Make a list of things you would like to improve. Check whether it would be easy or difficult to change them.

Things I would like to change	Easy to change	Difficult to change

2. For each day of the week, choose one positive change you could make to your lifestyle. Now try them!

   At the end of the week, record how successful you were in achieving these changes.

	Change to be made	Successful?
Monday		
Tuesday		
Wednesday		
Thursday		
Friday		
Saturday		
Sunday		

HEALTH CHALLENGE

Work harder on one of the changes in Question 2 in which you were not as successful.